Mind, Fantasy & Healing

Mind, Fantasy & Healing

One woman's journey from conflict and illness to wholeness and health

ALICE HOPPER EPSTEIN

With an Introduction by Seymour Epstein, Ph.D.

Delacorte Press

Published by
Delacorte Press
Bantam Doubleday Dell Publishing Group, Inc.
666 Fifth Avenue
New York, New York 10103

Library of Congress Cataloging in Publication Data

Epstein, Alice Hopper.
    Mind, fantasy, and healing: one woman's journey from conflict
and illness to wholeness and health / Alice Hopper Epstein; with an
introduction by Seymour Epstein.
        p. cm.
    ISBN 0-385-29712-2
    1. Epstein, Alice Hopper—Health. 2. Cancer—Patients—United
States—Biography. 3. Psychosynthesis. 4. Imagery (Psychology)—
Therapeutic use. 5. Cancer—Psychological aspects. I. Title.
RC265.6.E67A3   1989
362.1'9699'4—dc19
[B]   88-36606
                                                                   CIP
Manufactured in the United States of America
Published simultaneously in Canada
June 1989
10 9 8 7 6 5 4 3 2 1

BG

This book is dedicated to Sy, Didi, and all of my helpers, and especially to the "little girl with the red wagon."

Acknowledgments

In April 1985 my physician told me that I had incurable cancer and that I probably would not live for more than three months. His dire predictions never came true, because now—four years later—I am whole in body and spirit.

The process of regaining my health sent me on a fascinating journey into my mind. On all inner quests we journey alone, we fight dragons alone, and we win or die alone. But in this essential separateness we move through a landscape populated with others who urge us on, stop us for exquisite moments of intimacy, or guide us with their knowledge. So it was for me, and so I want to acknowledge my myriad helpers.

From my husband, Sy, came the rationale of why I was sick and the faith that I could cure myself. He did not believe in miracles, but as a clinical psychologist and expert on emotions and stress, he was sure that if I could change my fundamental assumptions and attitudes, my immune system would respond and I would be well. Finally, he told me that although he knew that he would survive if I died, he loved me dearly and was ready to make any sacrifice needed for my recovery.

From my daughter Lisa came another kind of strength.

She told me that she was not prepared for me to die and that I had better do something about it. The first step—and the most essential one in her mind—was to think in healthy terms. She wrote an affirmation for me which I repeated during my meditations. She found readings for me that I am convinced contributed to my recovery, and, most important, she led me to my therapist, Dorothy (Didi) Firman.

It was from Didi that I learned the method of psychosynthesis. She taught me to be strong in the world, to follow the instincts of my higher self, and she trained me to use my fantasy life to fight the monsters in my mind. Didi was the most attentive listener I have ever known. She never promised me that I would live, only that I would be whole. The journey to synthesis became so absorbing that within a few weeks I almost forgot that I was fighting for my life.

The contributions of my daughter Marty and son-in-law Toby were of a different nature. From Marty I received incredible love and emotional support. But also, at a crucial time in my recovery, together they provided me with a critical reprieve. Their independent investigation of an alternative interferon program made me consider the best physical therapy and not just grasp the first one that was available. But most important, the distraction of decision-making bought me the precious time during which my own psychospiritual healing could manifest itself.

My sister, Ruth, and her family (Don, Donna, and Jon) played an important role from near and afar. She helped to take care of me when I returned from the hospital, sent me tapes to enhance my visualizations of health, and prayed constantly for my recovery. She aggressively goaded me to consider the negative aspects of my most basic attachments. I got worse before I got better, but in the process I recovered.

Stewart, my husband's nephew, also believed in the

power of prayer. As a devotee of the Hindu guru Parmahansa Yogananda, he became a powerful force in my self-healing. He introduced me to the Hindu ideas about the relationship between mind and body and taught me some of the meditation tools that allowed me to reach into my essential being for the strength to initiate change.

Anna, Stewart's sister, taught me about openness and the power to heal. She sent me the plaque with a prescription for change that I kept near me while I meditated. It read, "Desire. Belief. Gratitude. Expect a Miracle." I asked; I believed; I was grateful; and the miracle happened.

Stewart and Anna's mother, Gerry, and their brother, Josh, also gave me wonderful support. From Gerry, my husband's sister-in-law, came the first new relationship for my changed self. We shared similar experiences of dealing with grief and pain. From Josh came much needed encouragement in the form of beautiful postcards from Hawaii.

Besides my close family, there were friends who helped me in special ways: Lynn Robinson, Annette Maxberry, Sylvia and Ervin Staub, Morrie and Sophie Ditch, Helene and her husband, Dr. Murthy, Florence Bert, Carol Shedoyan, Ann and George Levinger, Judy and Jim Averill, Rachel and Icek Aizen, Eva and Shelly Cashdan. They became members of our extended family, sharing our worst fears and our final triumph.

I would also like to express thanks to my innumerable physicians: Dr. Roger K. Miller, my surgeon, who treated me with great skill, candor, and respect, Dr. Gillian H. Chandran, Dr. Marc S. Ernstoff, Drs. Garnick and Kosty, Dr. Robert Rechtschaffen and therapist Peggy Roggenbuck, Dr. Willard T. Weeks, our longtime physician and friend, Dr. Thomas R. Weil, and Dr. Garry Reiter.

Finally, there were other invisible presences that were helping me too. Courageous health workers such as Carl

Simonton, Stephanie Matthews-Simonton, Norman Cousins, and Bernie Siegel were among the many experts who believed in the power of the mind to heal and gave hints on how one might proceed. I was influenced by all those pioneers who had preceded me; without their guidance I would have been much more hesitant to begin.

I believe that my physicians healed my body as best they could and without the spiritual and psychological help that I received I would not be the person I am today. I gladly acknowledge my debt to you all for my second chance.

I want to thank my husband, Sy, for his help in reading every page of the manuscript, for making many useful suggestions, and for continuous discussions about all aspects of the book. I also appreciate his help and that of my daughters, Lisa and Marty, and of Lynn Robinson, and George and Ann Levinger in reworking the title.

I am grateful to my editor, Robert Miller, for his efforts in creating the perfect cover for the book and for his advice to cut, cut, cut and then to cut some more. I gave up many fantasies and dreams grudgingly, but the story is stronger as a result.

Alice Hopper Epstein, Ph.D.
Amherst, Massachusetts
June 1989

Contents

Introduction
Seymour Epstein, Ph.D.

WHAT THIS BOOK IS ABOUT

This book can be viewed from three perspectives: as a fairy tale, as a journey into the mind, and as an account of an ordinary human being's struggle with cancer. At its simplest level it is a fairy tale, replete with evil witches, wise but treacherous snakes, flying horses, kindly elephants, and a pathetic, hobbling crab (the very symbol of cancer) who dreams of being a flying horse but is transformed, instead, into a beautiful bird that freely soars and sings a magnificent song. Above all it is the story of "Baby Alice," the heroine of the piece, who starts out as a helpless baby who has to be taken care of but winds up as more than a match for all the demons combined. Almost all fairy tales describe life-and-death encounters. This one is no exception. It differs, however, in one important respect. In ordinary fairy tales the life that hangs in the balance is that of a fictitious hero or heroine. We identify with the heroes and heroines of the stories we read, suffer with them in their tribulations, and rejoice with them in their victories. Yet all the while we know in the back of our minds that they are make-believe. In the present story the life that is at stake is that of a real ɔn. As Baby Alice fares, so, we suspect, will fare the ʌl Alice.

The book also describes an incredible journey into the mind, a journey that will lead the voyager to new vistas. I am a research psychologist and a psychotherapist. For many years I have taught graduate and undergraduate courses on theories of personality. I am very familiar with all the major theories of personality and most of the minor ones. For the past decade I have been developing my own theory of personality, one that integrates the major insights of other theories within a perspective that emphasizes the preconscious mind. I had reached a point where I was satisfied that my theory had finally resolved all the major dilemmas that had long puzzled me. This was before my wife's cancer and before I accompanied her, as one of her two therapists, on her incredible journey. I found that the map I carried was not only insufficient for charting the course, it was also insufficient for marking the roads we had traversed. Alice knew instinctively where we had to go, and I accepted her lead and followed. I was concerned that some of the demons she faced were better bypassed than confronted. It worried me that she would stir up feelings that would exacerbate her cancer. We had no time to waste, and it seemed to me there was no room for error. She reassured me that facing the demons of the past was necessary and, painful as it was, the pain was of a different quality from the feelings of helplessness and self-negation that we both believed lay at the root of her illness.

Freudians, Jungians, Adlerians, and other psychotherapists, including adherents of psychosynthesis, the form of therapy practiced so well and to such advantage by Didi Firman, Alice's other therapist, no doubt will all find grist for their mill in the data that are presented. However, if they are not completely doctrinaire, I believe they will also find, as I did, that there remains grist that their mills cannot grind. The observations of what took place in Alice's mind caused me to revise my thinking about how the mind works. It convinced me that there is a level of knowledge that is not conscious but is also not as deeply repressed and resistant to exploration as Freud and Jung would have it. At this level the mind stores and retrieves information, in part, in the form of metaphor and visual image. It does so not necessarily to protect the conscious mind from anxiety, as Freud maintained (although I do not doubt that this also occurs), but because that is its basic manner of operation. It is a mind that is no less adaptive than our conscious, rational mind, but it adapts to life through the medium of its own language and manner of apprehending reality. It employs metaphor and imagery in preference to word and number, and it connects events according to their emotional significance rather than their logical coherence. I believe this level of mind is intimately related to mood, emotion, intuition, and body functioning.

There are many therapies today that utilize visualization as a means of deconditioning anxiety and providing an active orientation to fighting disease by counteracting feelings of helplessness and depression. As useful as these techniques are, I believe they but scratch the surface. Yet more powerful is the ability of the mind to automatically encode experience, organize it, direct our behavior, and assess where we stand and where we are going in our lives, and it does this continuously and unconsciously. If we can learn to understand how this aspect of mind functions, and to integrate its wisdom with that from our conscious minds, I believe it could profoundly affect the quality of our lives, including our physical well-being.

Most of us regard ourselves as highly rational beings. Unfortunately, too often we do so by denying aspects of our emotions and intuitive thought processes. In the process we become alienated from our innermost experience. To deny a part of ourselves that actually exists in the name of rationality is, of course, the height of irrationality.

A third perspective from which the book can be viewed is in terms of what it has to offer about the relation of mind to physical illness. It is, of course, not possible from a single case to determine the generality of what was observed. It would be simplistic from the kind of evidence presented here, and for that matter anywhere, to assume that all cases of cancer involve a major psychological component and can be treated by psychological means, either by itself or in conjunction with more conventional medical treatment. However, it is equally unreasonable to assume that Alice's case is unique. Certainly there must be others like her, people for whom the psychological component in their illness has played a major role. If this book can inspire one such person to take steps that will save or improve one additional life, it will have more than justified its existence. A related contribution would be for her story to stimulate students of medicine and psychology to take seriously the power of the mind to hinder and facilitate the healing process, and to translate this interest into the practice of healing and the conduct of research. It is through such procedures that the quality and quantity of many lives can be improved.

HOW IT ALL BEGAN

I will never forget that day in April 1985 when we learned Alice had cancer. The experience of facing her imminent death, of mobilizing to fight the cancer, and of finally defeating it against all odds radically transformed her, produced significant changes in me, and opened up to both of us an appreciation of the awesome power of the subconscious mind to produce a hell or heaven on earth.

I remember with equal poignancy a day shortly thereafter when Alice and I went for our daily walk on one of the trails in the woods near our house. There was new snow on the ground and a crispness to the air. It was a dazzling, invigorating day that under other circumstances would have caused our hearts to leap with joy. I looked at Alice and saw tears rolling down her cheeks. I put my arm around her and asked what was on her mind. Choking with sobs, she said, "It is the last snow I will ever see!" She continued to weep in silence for a while. Then, suddenly, a transformation came over her that startled me. A fierce anger welled up in her, and she said with determination, "I am not going to die! I will fight it. I will fight it with everything I have, and I will defeat it." I was shocked at the intensity of her reaction. I told her I would do everything I could to help her, no matter what. Everything we owned and all my time would be at her disposal. If it would help, I would take a leave of absence from my position as a professor, and we would sell the house if we needed the money. I then said I was impressed with how much she did not want to die, but I would like to hear more about why she wanted to live. It shocked her when she was unable to come up with anything of significance. What came to mind was the thought that she did not really have very much to live for, and that perhaps everyone would be better off if she were dead. She told me, "You will be able to turn me in for a better model, a younger, more attractive woman." I embraced her and told her that I did not want another model, that I was very happy with the one I had. I thought to myself, *My God, how can she feel so unloved when her children, so many others, and I repeatedly demonstrate in deed as well as word how much we care for her?*

And so the battle was joined. On one side was the fierce determination to overcome whatever obstacles might be and to live. And not only to live, but to soar unfettered into space with a newfound freedom. On the other side were the demons of the mind that rose out of the graves of buried childhood memories to hiss their message that Alice was unlovable and guilty and deserved to die. The odds on the outcome were four against a thousand in favor of the demons. The chapters that follow describe the engagements that ensued.

PSYCHOLOGICAL FACTORS IN CANCER

The cancer from which Alice suffered was a kidney cancer, more technically known as a hypernephroma. We were informed that the left kidney contained a large tumor, the size of a lemon, but, if we were lucky, the cancer would be confined to the kidney, which could be removed. We weren't lucky. X rays revealed the cancer had spread to one of the lungs. It was decided to remove the kidney anyway and then remove part of the lung if the cancer did not spread farther during a one-month observation period. Again, luck failed us. The cancer not only spread to another site in the same lung but to the other lung as well. An operation to remove part of one lung was no longer feasible. No promising medical treatment remained. We were told that we could try an experimental interferon treatment program if we wished, but that the odds were not very good. Our home physician informed us that it would be just as reasonable to do nothing. We were told by the oncologist that, at the rate the cancer was spreading, Alice could not be expected to live more than three months. Alice was seriously considering the interferon treatment despite the unpleasant side effects that she knew she might experience. At the same time I began to read everything I could about alternative forms of treatment. I was amazed to learn that some authorities believed that psychological factors played an important role in both the etiology of, and recovery from, cancer. We read the book *Getting Well Again,* by the Simontons, and listened to their tapes. A new dimension of understanding was opened up to us and, with it, a new source of hope.

Throughout history there have been reports of spontaneous remissions from cancer that defied medical wisdom. Many of these have consisted of faith healings, such as cases recorded at the shrine at Lourdes. I do not believe in miracles, but I know that beliefs and the emotions associated with them can have an important effect on the functioning of the body, which is all that is necessary to understand why faith healing works. I learned that there is a rapidly developing new field of science called psychoneuroimmunology, which is devoted to the study of relations between mind, neurology, and the immune system. I further learned that the most widely accepted theory of cancer is that it is produced by a relative failure of the immune system, either because it is overwhelmed or because it is deficient. Everyone regularly produces cancer cells, but our immune system normally destroys the cancer cells as rapidly as they are produced. When for some reason the capacity of the immune system is reduced or the immune system is overwhelmed by carcinogenic agents beyond its ability to control, people come down with cancer. I read of human as well as animal research that implicated stress and depression as sources of immuno-suppression. A case report that particularly interested me was one that described a person who had received a kidney transplant that contained latent cancer cells. Once the person's immune system was suppressed, which was necessary to keep the kidney from being rejected, cancer spread like wildfire through his body. The physicians then discontinued the immuno-suppression, and within a matter of weeks the person was entirely free of cancer. True, it was only a single case, but it provided a dramatic demonstration of the power of the immune system to remove cancer.

Putting all the evidence together, the following conclusion about the role of psychological factors in cancer seemed reasonable to me. Psychological factors can influence the endocrine and immune systems and therefore can influence susceptibility to, and recovery from, cancer. Psychological factors are but one set of factors among others, and it is not clear what their relative importance is. It is well established that environmental agents, diet, heredity, and certain diseases can influence cancer. Compared to these other factors, psychological ones may be trivial. However, I was not concerned with abstractions based on averages over many people. I was interested in understanding a specific case, and it seemed self-evident that any particular factor might exert a greater or lesser influence, depending on the case in question. Accordingly, I formed the hypothesis that psychological factors are of minor significance in some cases, of moderate significance in many, and of major significance in others. I concluded that the most sensible approach to the treatment of Alice's cancer was to use all available approaches, as long as they could do no harm. There seemed to be nothing to lose and much to gain by adding improved diet and a psychological approach to whatever standard medical procedures were available, of which there were none with real promise.

What made me most hopeful about employing a psychological approach was that my wife fit the description of the "cancer-prone personality" to an amazing degree. On the surface Alice was cheerful, helpful to others, highly competent, and much loved by many people in and out of the family. The only one who did not love her was herself. She could do things for others, but she could not do things for herself, nor could she accept favors from others, nor, apparently, could she even accept the fact that others loved her. Her manifest enthusiasm and cheerfulness masked an underlying depression. It seemed to me that, if in her case personality had played an important role in the etiology of the cancer, then changing her personality could contribute to her recovery. Thus, if anyone could benefit from a psychological approach, it made sense that it would be someone with a cancer-prone personality, like Alice.

Alice resolved to change her attitude toward living, to learn to appreciate each day, and to make her remaining time as meaningful and authentic as possible. A quest for self-understanding and improvement became the focus of her life from that point on. She now says that cancer is the best thing that ever happened to her because it forced her to reorganize her personality. It is important to understand that she was not trying so much to defeat the cancer but to become the person she wanted to be, not someone whom she believed others wanted her to be. She was completely involved in this task, which she felt was the most important thing she could do with her life. Thus there was no problem with feeling the cancer was her fault, or that she should feel guilty if she failed to defeat it. No matter what the outcome, it made sense to her to make the most of what time remained.

I cannot overemphasize the dedication with which Alice applied herself in her quest for self-understanding and becoming the kind of person she wanted to be. She undertook intensive psychotherapy, and, fortunately, found an excellent therapist who was extremely well suited to her. She meditated and did visualization exercises daily, and she

opened herself up to people in a way that was completely
new to her and would be for most people. She took from
others with appreciation and without guilt, and she learned
with amazement that they loved her all the more for it. She
worked on overcoming her anger and anxiety and on becoming a more appreciative, loving, assertive, and self-ac-
cepting person. The result was that she began to change
psychologically, and with the psychological changes came
some remarkable physical changes. For example, Alice
never used to sweat. As a result she had been unable to play
tennis in hot weather, as she would get overheated. Suddenly Alice began to sweat when she exerted herself in hot
weather. Something different was apparently going on with
her hormones. Relatedly, as we were soon to discover,
something important was happening with her immune system, for her tumors had begun to shrink.

Alice had explored participating in the experimental interferon program at the Dana Farber Clinic in Boston, but
then decided on the Yale–New Haven Clinic. Immediately
before the first interferon treatment in New Haven, X rays
had to be taken to provide a baseline against which future
changes could be evaluated. The X rays revealed such a
dramatic decrease in the tumors compared to those taken a
month before in Amherst that we decided to postpone treatment to see if the progress would continue. We certainly did
not wish to begin anything new that might jeopardize the
progress she was making. The progress continued, and the
chief oncologist agreed that, under the circumstances, there
was no point in initiating interferon treatment. He told us
that he had never seen a case like Alice's in the history of
Yale–New Haven Clinic, which is a major clinic with a divi-
sion specializing in kidney cancer. I called the chief oncologist at the Dana Farber Clinic, and he, too, said he had
never seen such a case in his experience. I wrote to the

National Cancer Institute, and they sent me photocopies of research studies on the course of metastasized kidney cancer. In one study of 141 patients with metastasized kidney cancer, including 33 whose affected kidney had been removed, there was none who survived beyond two years (see Bibliography, Middleton). Following a review of studies of mortality in patients with metastasized kidney cancer, a respected medical textbook on cancer (see Bibliography, DeVita, Hellman, and Rosenberg) concluded that the incidence of regression is probably less than four in one thousand. It also reported that there is no evidence that removal of the kidney after the cancer has metastasized prolongs life.

By now Alice has been free of detectable signs of cancer for three years. Of course we have no guarantee about what the future holds. It is possible that the cancer will someday return. Yet, even if it does, the progress up to this point would have to be considered remarkable. It is also possible that what Alice did was only coincidentally related to the regression of her cancer. One reason I suspect this is not the case is that the progress of the cancer varied with Alice's activities. During a period of a few weeks when she abandoned her program to make arrangements for our daughter's wedding, I feared the growth of the tumors would resume. Fortunately, this did not occur, but neither did the steady shrinkage that had occurred up to that time continue. When she went back to her program the tumors again began to shrink.

What are the implications of my wife's experience for others who suffer from cancer? I am aware that the form of psychological treatment she employed is not suitable for everyone. I believe there are other approaches that can also be effective. The important thing to be accomplished in any case where psychological factors play an important role is to produce an enduring change in mood. For those with a cancer-prone personality, a basic change in attitude toward self and life may be necessary. For others a change in situation or life-style, new commitments in work or love, religious devotion, or some other kind of faith may make the difference. Unfortunately, where changes involve events and others, they cannot always be relied on. Where changes involve the self, this is another matter, for one is always free to work at understanding and improving one's attitudes about self and others in a manner that will make life as rewarding as possible.

Physicians frequently have reservations about a psychological approach to the treatment of cancer, even when employed in conjunction with standard medical practice, because they believe it fosters guilt. The argument they present is that informing patients that psychological factors can play a role in the etiology of cancer and can influence recovery from it will make people feel responsible both for getting ill and for not improving. This is said to be an awful thing to do to people who have already suffered a great deal and do not need the added burden of feeling guilty. This argument against a psychological approach is no more reasonable than an argument against advising patients to improve their diet because it implies that poor diet brought on the cancer, which could cause them to feel guilty. Extended to its logical conclusion, the argument is against trying to do anything of significance when the outcome is less than certain, because if one tries and fails, one will feel guilty for having failed.

The essence of the problem is not that one may attempt to affect the course of one's illness and fail, but that one may inappropriately blame oneself if one's efforts do not succeed. Improvements in diet, chemotherapy, or psychological work may or may not be effective. When this is accepted one can reasonably work at maximizing the odds of recovery by doing all that is reasonable. If the procedure is likely to enhance the quality of life, then it is a good bargain, for there is nothing to lose and something to gain. If one blames oneself for doing the best that one can to no avail, then the answer is not to avoid taking action but to identify the maladaptive thoughts and reject them.

It is important to recognize that psychological factors are but one of many that may contribute to the etiology and course of cancer. Thus it makes little sense to assume that one's emotions and attitudes necessarily "caused" the cancer. Yet in any one case it remains a possibility that they contributed to the cancer, and as long as it does it is worth exploring whether psychological changes can be helpful. Moreover, even if psychological factors played no role in the etiology of the disease, it is still reasonable to do everything one can to put one's body in the best position to combat it, which includes achieving the best possible state of mental health.

Some physicians object to a psychological approach because they fear it will produce "false hope." I have never quite understood what false hope is. All hope is "false" in the sense that what is hoped for may not materialize. At the time of hoping one cannot know the outcome. If the hope serves to improve one's quality of life and does not cause one to avoid taking adaptive action when it is possible, nor be resentful when the hoped-for outcome does not materialize, then it is obviously desirable. The problem is not with hoping—it is with demanding guaranteed results. Could one fault my wife for having had unreasonable hope in believing that she could defeat her cancer against all odds? One should judge an act by its likely consequences. What it led her to do was to work very hard at becoming psychologically whole: at replacing feelings of disappointment and resentment with feelings of appreciation and love; at replacing a self-sacrificial attitude and its associated feelings of help-lessness with one that fostered self-assertion and respect for her own needs; and, finally, of replacing self-negation and inner conflict with wholeness and inner harmony. This for her was a worthy, satisfying endeavor no matter what the ultimate outcome of the disease. It would have been a worthwhile task if she did not have cancer. Had she lived only three or six months, it is hard to imagine a better, more fulfilling way she could have spent her time. As matters turned out, it contributed, we believe, to saving her life, which, from the perspective she took, was a most wonderful bonus.

Seymour Epstein, Ph.D.
Professor of Psychology
University of Massachusetts at Amherst

Mind, Fantasy & Healing

PART I

The Self-Destructive Mind

1

Darkening Reality

The mind that heals also has the power to destroy. In my experience the process of self-healing and of self-destruction were similar but opposite ways of being in the world. So, in order to tell the whole story of how I recovered from cancer, I must begin with how I became ill.

There are two prevalent theories connecting life events and psychological reactions to the onset of cancer, and I believe that I fit both of them. The first and more acceptable idea is that cancer is frequently preceded by a traumatic loss or stressful situation that reduces the functioning of the body's immune system. The theory is supported by human as well as animal studies which show that laboratory-induced stress reduces the immune reaction. In February of 1983, two years before the onset of my illness, I was in a very stressful situation while studying for my preliminary exams for a Ph.D. I did not suffer an objective loss at this time: no one died or left me, and I did not fail my exam. However, the process was a painful one for me because I did not perform at the very high level that I had set for myself. Even when I finally received my degree I took no pride or pleasure in the accomplishment. What should have been a moment of triumph became a time of despair.

In order to understand how in my mind I turned a success into a "failure" and then into a depression that, I suspect, contributed to my life-threatening illness, I have to turn to the other, more controversial theory about cancer, that of a cancer-prone personality. I fit that theory too. I believe that I fit it perfectly.

One of the reasons that some laymen and physicians are skeptical about the psychological precursors of cancer is that not everyone who is under stress or suffers loss develops the disease. In order to account for this inconsistency, the idea of a cancer-prone personality was introduced. According to this theory, people who react to stressful situations by feeling helpless and hopeless or tend not to express emotions are more susceptible to cancer because their losses have special meaning to them and their personalities make them less able to cope with the loss. People who supposedly are prone to cancer have other interesting sets of traits. They are extremely sympathetic and helpful to others and find it hard to express anger, but they are also often extremely critical of themselves and frequently belittle their accomplishments. Although to others they appear competent and successful, in their own estimations they are helpless and out of control. The most problematic aspect of this syndrome is that they have a very weak sense of self.

Until recently there was no known connection between these characteristics and the immune system, making the theory very suspect. Recently, however, studies have demonstrated that feelings of helplessness and depression also affect the immune system. While this book can neither prove nor disprove either of the theories of cancer, I will assume that they played a major role in my illness because the correspondence between my life events and my reactions to them so closely followed the ideas that I have described. Essentially what I am saying is: If stressful events trigger cancer, and if a cancer-prone personality plays a role in coping with the stress, this book will describe the way certain events and attitudes may be translated into illness. Just as important to this statement is a very hopeful corollary: A disease that is brought on by psychological stress may be turned around by the psychological methods that worked for me.

How did I begin my descent into inner turmoil and a life-threatening sickness? The story begins before I became ill, even before the time of studying for my exams. Even though I appeared to be a happy, outgoing, and confident person, the seeds of self-negativity were always present in my desire to please others and in my willingness to sacrifice my needs to theirs. Years of living and reacting consistent with these characteristics slowly robbed me of my confidence, made me obsessed with my imagined failures, and made me incapable of accepting the love that was all around me.

One very destructive path that I followed was in my professional life. I made several important decisions that led me out of my original profession as a mathematics teacher and into a Ph.D. program in sociology at the University of Massachusetts. I went step by step making choices that were not self-fulfilling.

In the beginning I loved to teach. From my early days of teaching dancing at summer camp to being a graduate assistant at the University of Wisconsin, I had a reputation as a creative and compassionate teacher. "You make math seem more like fun than studying," my students would tell me. What I did not tell them—but what they probably guessed —is that it was fun for me too.

My career was also a major source of self-esteem for me. By the time I was twenty-two I had a master's degree in mathematics and had completed teacher training. I was proud of the fact that I could continue my career by teaching in local colleges while I was raising my two daughters,

Lisa and Marty. I was pleased to be able to supplement our family income at a time when my husband, Sy, was underpaid as a young professor.

As time went on, however, I developed a great deal of ambivalence about my teaching. There were problems with finding baby-sitters or live-in help to relieve me of my household duties. There were constant conflicts between the time I devoted to preparation and the time I could spend in recreation with Sy and the children. This was a problem particularly during the two years that I taught at Amherst High School, and eventually I left this job and returned to teaching at the university, where my time was more flexible. I believe that this decision was a mistake, because I gave up a job for which I was well trained and in which I could express my creative abilities. I should have worked harder at solving the problems at home.

At first the university teaching was good because it was only part-time. But I missed the high school and found the students at the university were becoming disinterested and rebellious. In addition, with only a master's degree, I could never hope to get tenure or promotions. I began to change, to detest my job, and to develop strange, unproductive attitudes about myself. Compliments about my teaching would often distress me, especially if students indicated that they preferred me to other members of the staff. Once I became irrationally angry when Sy told me about parents who had stopped him on the street with stories of how much their children had enjoyed being in my class. The praise didn't seem warranted to me. I began to feel that I was not better than other teachers, only that I was willing to work harder than most. In my mind, if you had to work so hard for something, it didn't count.

The final outcome of my discontent was that I gave up teaching and embarked on a career of volunteer work to help save the natural resources of our town. In 1968 the University of Massachusetts was in a period of incredible growth and Amherst was being graced with a thousand new apartments a year. I decided that I would not return to work for a while and that I would try to do something about the local issues that were facing us. This was my second mistake, because my desire to help save Amherst was an excuse. I was afraid to return to teaching because I knew that the old conflicts would return if I did.

At first my life as a volunteer was rewarding. In short time I became a town-meeting member and then chair of the Amherst Planning Board. We successfully blocked runaway development. But once again my commitments began to interfere with my life at home and I began to look for new avenues for my energies. I decided to follow my newly developed skills as a planner, and so I returned to school and received a master's degree in regional planning. But I was not confident in my ability as a planner. I felt that I was too old to apply for planning jobs. Perhaps I was still afraid of a full-time career commitment. At any rate, I decided that I would continue in school for a Ph.D. I was accepted in two top-notch Ph.D. programs in planning, one at Harvard and one at Cornell.

As the time for making my final plans arrived, both Sy and I realized that either alternative would mean a big change in our lives. We were home alone now: Lisa was in Boston and Marty was starting graduate school at Penn State. If I went to either of the schools that had accepted me, it would mean long periods of separation. Sy and I had always had a close relationship. We talked incessantly about our mutual work and interests and we spent most of our free time with each other. I decided at the last minute that I was not ready to go to either school and so I applied to and was accepted by the sociology department at the University of Massachusetts. I believed that a degree in Urban Sociology would be a reasonable substitute for a planning degree. What I didn't understand at the time was that I was again sacrificing my basic needs at the altar of relationship. This was my third poor decision, and it was the beginning of my course down and then out.

It was not obvious at first that I had made a mistake. By outward standards I was a successful student: I had good grades and a fellowship that allowed me to do my own research. But as time went on I felt more and more like an outsider; in my own mind, the experience became less and less rewarding. I kept emphasizing my weak points and downplaying my strengths. Although I learned to write research reports and to analyze data statistically, I was absolutely lacking in confidence to get an academic job. The sum of my years of professional experience and training was that I was much less secure and confident than I had been as a beginning teacher in Wisconsin.

Parallel to the unhappy path of my professional life was the way I convinced myself that my relationship with Sy was at risk. I began to be uncomfortable when he spent time with his young and attractive graduate students. But my feelings of insecurity became particularly acute during the year the family spent in Switzerland while Sy was on sabbatical leave from the University of Massachusetts. It should have been an ideal year for all of us. We lived in a beautiful house in a tiny hamlet high in the Swiss Alps. Sy worked on writing several research papers, the children attended a local private school, and we hiked or skied every day depending on the season. For me, however, the isolation, the language barrier, and the separation from my usual sources of self-esteem were devastating. I became extremely jealous about innocent attentions he paid to one of our friends. We spent many hours trying to understand why I an event of world-shaking proportions. The exam became one final test of my abilities, one final challenge that I knew I could not win. I call this the mentality of the "last report card." I believe it is an exaggerated illustration of a cancer-prone personality hard at work at self-destruction.

I suspect that the attitude of the last report card may be characteristic of other "cancer-prone" individuals when faced with difficult situations or severe loss. A loss itself would be hard for anyone, but those who are cancer-prone may complicate the situation by interpreting it in personal terms and using it to justify their feelings of inadequacy. But even more important, the stressful event may highlight a fear that is more terrifying than a lack of self-worth. In my case I began to realize to my horror—that there was no self inside me except the self that worked for A's on tests. If I failed, my life would become unbearable. I would know for sure that I was an empty shell.

was so sensitive, and eventually the feeling w
However, under what appeared to be a loving rela
often felt that I could not trust him to look ou
welfare. On the other hand, I was fearful about an
ing him and often would mask my dissatisfaction b
especially affectionate. From his perspective he sensec
would often express unexpected feelings of disconten
he didn't understand what he could do to please me.

These two roads of self-negativity converged as the
arrived for me to take my preliminary exams. It seemed ı
the more I studied, the more tense I became. After a wh
year of preparation, I was a month away from my exam aı
climbing the walls. My tension was palpable, my speech wa
halting. I was touchy, quick to anger, and just plain scared.
Both Sy and I knew that I had to do something about my
tension level, but what concerned him even more was the
strange self-negating attitude that I was developing about
the experience of studying for my exams. I began to recall
my early school days and how tense I had always been in
the classroom. I bemoaned the fact that I had always been
an overachiever who believed that I had to get A's in order
to be loved. I viewed the coming exam as some final test of
my worth, a test that I knew I could not pass. When I was
in a calmer, more rational mood, Sy would often ask me to
try to understand where these beliefs were coming from. I
would turn on him, deny that I was being hard on myself,
and accuse him of trying to treat me like a patient. In other
words, when I was out of my self-punitive mood, I could
not understand what he was worried about.

One evening he asked me if he could record one of our
discussions. He wanted me to hear myself when I was in a
negative mood. I agreed reluctantly and he taped the session
that you will read in the next chapter. Although in reality I
was facing the stress from a coming test, in my mind it was

2

"The Last Report Card"

We all have periods of tension in our lives, times when we feel we can't go on. Yet we do. We live through the tense period; we do not develop a serious illness. What was unique about my struggle with taking my exam was the concomitant self-destructive attitude that developed at this time, which—by my refusing to seek some outside help—was subsequently nurtured until it permeated my whole existence.

One morning about a month before my exam all the fears and frustrations of years of graduate school came to a head. Sy took me aside after breakfast and asked me to talk to him about the situation. He was worried because, as a clinical psychologist he recognized that I was becoming extremely tense.

"Tense," I cried out. "Of course I'm tense. I—"

Before I could make any excuses he said, "Okay, that's my point, Alice, you can't go on like this; we have to do something about it. Let's see what is really involved in this exam for you."

Sitting down and controlling the tears that I knew were close, I carefully punctuated each word, speaking slowly and distinctly. "What's involved is that I hate taking tests. I hate getting grades. Ever since the first grade I've been afraid to get my report card."

"Alice, knowing you, I'm sure that you could take the exam today and pass," he said.

This last statement infuriated me so much that I stood up and started to pace the floor. "Oh, don't start that," I screamed. "You don't understand. I could forget everything. I could go so completely blank that I would make a complete fool of myself. You—"

"But you probably won't," he interrupted. "You're just afraid you will. It—"

I turned abruptly. Putting both hands up in front of me as a signal that he must stop, I cried out, "Sy, listen to me. Listen! I've painted myself into a corner. I have no place to turn. I feel that all the report-card times have been condensed into one, one last exam, one last evaluation. Sy, this may truly be my last report card!"

With this remark I burst into tears. Terrible sobs came from deep inside me. I reached for the Kleenex box; it was empty. I went over to the kitchen counter to get more. When I returned Sy was sitting in the same place waiting for me. At that moment our younger dog, Chaya, who had been in the room all the time, rolled over on her back and let out a strange sound like a moan. We both laughed, I mostly at myself for my ludicrous behavior. I laughed and cried some more and went over to Sy and put my head on his shoulder. The angry spell was broken, but the fear remained. We agreed to continue the discussion so that we could understand what about the last report card was so hard for me to handle.

That evening we sat down again in the living room, where we hold our serious talks. Sy said, "Let's try to capture your feelings of this morning. Let's try to imagine that you have failed. What happens?"

I sighed deeply as I imagined coming home after having flunked my exam. I could feel the emotion welling up in me. I could feel the tension in my mouth as I started again: "Well . . . ah . . . ah . . . well . . . I would have to face you and Marty and Lisa. I'd have to tell everybody that I failed. My sister . . ."

"And what do you think we would say? Do you think we would relate to you differently? Would we reject you?"

"No."

"Would we be sympathetic?" he questioned.

"Yes . . . yes but . . ." I paused and started to tap my finger on the nearby table. Suddenly becoming more certain and bolder in my speech, I retorted, "I don't care what anyone will think or how you all feel. I only care about how *I* will feel."

I knew that I was losing control now, and as I felt my emotions taking over I cried out, "I don't want to hear any more. You don't understand. I'm telling you I won't stay here if I fail. I couldn't." I was sobbing now, deep sobs and halting breath.

Sy remained calm as always, sympathizing but still not letting me get too lost in the emotion as he probed with his comments. "These are strong irrational feelings, aren't they? Notice what happens when we debunk your view that the world will reject you. It is an automatic reaction, a flare of emotion. Aren't you saying 'No matter how the world reacts, I'll react negatively. I'll be intolerant and miserable to myself'? There is something in you that makes you not want to believe that you can fail and still be loved. It's probably a reaction from the past. Logic tells you it is true that you can be, but you fight it."

Finally, getting control of myself, I managed to remark, "Well then, it must be deeper than I thought."

"Of course it's deeper," he agreed. "It's you who are intolerant of yourself, not us."

"Yes," I replied hoarsely, clearing my throat, "I'm afraid of people finding out what I am. But I'm most afraid that if I'm not successful in school, there's *nothing* to me."

"All there is to you is success in school?"

"Yes," I continued again. "I know that I'm not that good, but this would make it very clear to everyone, and then I would have nothing. Nothing."

As the significance of this confession struck home to me, I couldn't hold in the tears and I just cried and cried for several minutes until I knew that I couldn't take the intensity of the emotion anymore. We both agreed that our session should be over for the evening.

During the next day I took to heart what we had learned the day before—that I was my own worst enemy and that I was incredibly hard on myself. I took some constructive steps about the situation by trying to recall how my tension had begun.

I had always assumed that my nervousness in school was a result of the turmoil that existed in our household before and at the time I started first grade. In rapid succession three tragedies struck my family while I was growing up. When I was two and half years old my mother's twelve-year-old brother, Teddy, who was eighteen years her junior, died suddenly of unknown causes. One day he was a handsome, active boy, playing baseball and roller skating, and the next day he was dead. The shock was so great that my grandmother (Nana to me) had a "nervous breakdown," or what today would be considered severe depression. She was so distressed that she was sent away to the country to recuperate. Eventually she came out of the depression, but within a year after her recuperation she discovered that she had breast cancer.

My mother, who had always been close to her mother, refused to accept the verdict that Nana had only six months to live. She moved her into our home and proceeded to keep her busy by going places with us every day. We were an inseparable trio. As soon as the morning chores were finished, we were off to the mountains or to the seashore, shopping, anywhere just to keep going. One day we took off for Canada, which was a long trip on secondary roads. We stayed for several days and no one questioned what my mother was doing. She was able to postpone the inevitable for two years, but the inevitable did come.

It was an incredible six-month period in my life. In February of the year that my grandmother died, I started first grade. Since I would not be six years old until April, my mother thought that I was too young to attend school. She appealed to the school authorities to keep me home one more semester, saying that the walk was too long for me and involved crossing dangerous streets where there was no school guard. I remember vividly the day that the truant officer, in uniform, visited our house to tell her that she had to send me to school. It was frightening to hear them arguing over me and it made school sound like something terrible. In the end she complied with the regulations, but to assuage her fear she took me to and from school by car.

It was probably good that I was out of the house during these months because my grandmother suffered from intense pain as she neared death. My mother devoted herself and the household only to Nana and thought of no one else. What she failed to realize was that she should have been thinking about herself because she was pregnant. If one can believe the story as I remember it, my mother denied her condition until shortly before my sister was born at the end of May. Knowing my mother in her later years, and her way of putting unpleasant thoughts out of her mind, I believe she could have repressed her pregnancy. At any rate, I had absolutely no preparation for my sister's arrival.

The birth was hard on my mother, and for six weeks after my sister Ruth's birth, we had two patients in the household: my grandmother, dying of cancer, and my mother, ill and exhausted from childbirth and from concern over her mother's illness. The care of all of us, including the new baby, fell to Ella, our live-in maid. I have fond memories of the time she spent with me while she walked me back and forth to school. My mother regained her health, but by now my grandmother was bedridden and under the care of nurses who came on shifts night and day. It was a hectic time: people coming and going, the doctor, the nurses transported back and forth by my father. And then the frenzy came to an end when Nana died in August.

In September I started the second part of my first year at school. Even in first grade I was terrified that I wouldn't know the answers, afraid of people telling me that I had failed, of being embarrassed. I thought then that it was probably the insecurity resulting from what was going on at home. There was my mother's attention to her sick mother, my shock and rage at this new baby who came from nowhere, and finally the confusion over what happened to my grandmother when she died. No one ever explained anything to me.

But it was more than that. Before my grandmother's illness, and even after my sister's birth, my mother was extremely involved with me. In some sense she had transferred her ego to me. I was sent to dancing school at the age of three, put in dancing contests that I never liked nor could win. Oh, I came in second or third sometimes, but never the best. She took me for auditions for a kiddie show popular on the radio at the time. I had a small part once, but never the lead. I was dressed in little fur coats and short dresses so that I always looked different. Somehow this developed in me both a fear of failure and a great desire to succeed, especially to gain her approval and praise.

As I thought over this early history from an adult perspective, it became apparent that I never could be an ordinary person, make mistakes, be myself. There was always this need to be special, to be brilliant. Unfortunately, although I am good at a great many things, I am not brilliant. And now here I was pursuing the last report card, caught up in the impossible situation I had created for myself. I was aware now not only of the fear of the coming exam but also of the nagging fear that I was getting too old for this kind of strain, too old for this kind of trauma.

That evening, Sy and I talked about the events surrounding my sister's birth, and the deep sense of being wronged that I felt at that time. I wondered if my excessive worrying was connected with this event. Sy suggested that worrying may have been a way of giving me control in a world fraught with uncertainty. If I worried enough, bad things wouldn't happen: I would not fail, I would not be disapproved of, or perhaps no one would find out my darkest secrets, my unexpressed rage. He ended by saying, "Well, from what you're describing, what you're afraid of is a very frightening confrontation with a part of yourself, and I guess you ought to be aware that you can proceed at any rate that is useful to you."

Despite frequent prompting by Sy, even insistence on his part that we continue the conversation, this was the last time we talked about the last report card. Although I had promised to keep working on my self-destructive thinking, I didn't. I wouldn't even listen to the tape that Sy had made of the sessions because I tried to avoid the intense emotion of those evenings.

I managed to extinguish the brush fires that were ahead

of me with respect to my exam, but my negative thinking began to spread into all aspects of my interpersonal relations.

My daughter Marty was the first to bear the brunt of my growing sensitivity. No sooner had I dealt with my exams than the problem of Marty's coming marriage surfaced. Much to the surprise of us all, Marty was engaged to be married to a young man whom none of us liked or thought was right for her. He was the cantor of a large Jewish community in Wilmington, Delaware. She had left her job with Merrill Lynch in New York to take a job in Philadelphia to be near him and to prepare for their wedding. She, of necessity, was studying to convert to Judaism. This was a double shock that I found hard to handle.

Sy and I are from similar socioeconomic but different religious backgrounds. He is an atheist who is an ethnic Jew; I am a nonpracticing Protestant. We celebrated Christmas in a nonreligious way, and participated in the Jewish holidays when his relatives invited us to their celebrations. Our children were given no religious training, with the idea that they could choose for themselves when they got older.

This seemed fine with me, except that I never anticipated that either would be seriously interested in Judaism. Unfortunately, I interpreted Marty's action as a repudiation of my values and a personal rejection. I reacted to her, and she reacted back, and the very close relationship we previously had began to come apart. Sy and I finally agreed that we would go along with her decision and give her our full support, but not before much discussion and soul-searching on everyone's part . . . and excessive agony on mine. In the end Marty broke off the engagement just short of the wedding, but it was an emotional experience that was to leave its scars for some time.

I also began to feel insecure about myself with Sy and had

strange reactions to nice things that he did for me. Once he brought me a pair of earrings from a trip to Poland. I was thrilled with them until I realized that they were zircons and not diamonds. I launched into a tirade against him and felt terrible for days to think that the gift represented the level of his affection for me. I thought, *After all these years, this is what I'm worth to him—artificial diamonds.* It made no difference that he and my daughters bought me a pair of real diamond earrings and a necklace for the following Christmas. In my twisted mind, if you had to ask for a present, it didn't count for anything except obligation.

Thinking back to the time of the last report card, it is truly amazing to me now that I allowed myself to sink into such a morass of negative thinking, low self-esteem, and unhappiness when as a young girl and college student I had been enthusiastic, confident, and secure. In the eyes of most people who knew me, I still appeared to be so. People liked me because they knew that they could depend on me and because I was always so willing to listen, to see things from their viewpoint, and to be helpful in any way I could. I was good at getting people with different ideas together because I was adept at proposing compromises. I was effective in town meetings because my views were perceived as reasonable and because of my ability to present ideas clearly. Yet all of these strengths had their weak side as I derived little satisfaction from them and felt that I had to slight my own needs to fulfill the needs of others. I was smiling on the outside but hurting within.

The problematic aspects of my personality had started, I believe, with an inner sense, learned through years of early training, that I could not influence my personal environment by *direct behavior.* If situations were not to my liking, I had to make concessions. I had to give up what I wanted to appease first my mother and then Sy. It also made me look for and find devious ways of being in the world: to worry about things so they would not come about, to dwell on the negative side of things so I wouldn't be disappointed, and to have exaggerated dreams of personal relationships that were entirely unrealistic. Being passive was also devastating to my self-esteem and made life increasingly unsatisfying.

The same problematic approach led me to start the Ph.D. program. It was accepting my mother's standards for one final time. Many of us never give up our search for that chimera, that foolish fantasy, that one elusive achievement that will make everything right. My false dream was that getting a Ph.D. would bestow on me the self-esteem and autonomy that I lacked.

There was another more sinister and negative motive for obtaining the degree. It was as if at some level I said to myself, "Okay, you (meaning my mother) want me to do this? Fine. I'll show you. I'll do it with a vengeance. I'll kill myself in the process, and then you'll see what you have done to me." As the years in the program dragged on I had visions of dying so that people would feel guilty for how they had treated me. They (meaning my professors or Sy) would see how cruel they had been to me and they would be sorry. So the last report card was the culmination of a self-negating personality with a sense of flair. It was self-destruction on a grand scale, the last hurrah for the me that was motivated by other people. It was to be the explosion of a supernova.

The reason that I'm still alive and didn't self-destruct is that the little of the "real me" that was left fought back vigorously against the self-hostile part. This was the part of me that desperately wanted to be free. This was the part of me that had both the strength and dedication to living that finally saved me.

3

The Hollow Self

The personality that I described in the last chapter does not develop overnight. It begins in childhood and is shaped by years of interpretation of life's experiences. It is on a one-way street to destruction. Before going on with the consequences of these attitudes, I think it will be helpful to look at the details of how the cancer-prone personality is formed and how my early development followed these patterns. In making these connections I introduce a metaphor that helped to explain how the influences in my early life led to my self-negating behavior. I call this metaphor the "hollow self."

In *Love, Medicine, and Miracles,* Dr. Bernie Siegel gives a general explanation of how the cancer-prone personality is created and how it results in illness. He points out that patients who develop cancer after a loss often had a poor relationship with their parents and experienced conditional love. They react to their situation by trying hard to please their parents and others, and often life's meaning for these patients comes entirely from people and things outside of the self. This results in great dependency on others and a habit of putting the needs of others before their own. In other words, they buy affection by pleasing others rather than themselves. An understandable characteristic of such people is that they do not express anger because they cannot risk disapproval, let alone rejection. They cannot take credit for their own success and often feel inadequate in the face of accomplishment. Another result is that they develop exaggerated goals that they believe will bring them happiness. When they experience a loss they react with feelings of hopelessness and helplessness. The final step is the development of cancer.

But how are dependency and self-negation translated into hopelessness and helplessness? This is where the idea of the hollow self is helpful. According to psychologist Carl Rogers, part of the innate human drive toward actualization and growth involves the perception of oneself as a separate and distinct entity, which he calls the self-concept or self. He also posits that the most important element in the growth of the self is the presence of unconditional love.

I assume that unconditional love creates a background in which a child develops in its own right, learns from its mistakes, and takes pride in its accomplishments, thereby creating a solid core of self. Diagram A shows a visual image of the normal self with its solid, expanding core of self-esteem. Unconditional love directed to the child results in the child being able to love others in a healthy way and creates a sense of security that one is lovable. Accomplishment is converted into a feeling of control of the environment, and empathy for others leads to positive feelings about the self as good and caring. The power of this sense of one's own entity is that needs can be identified and satisfied, fears can be expressed and conquered, hopes can be modulated and turned into accomplishments. Through this process the child gains *direct* control over its environment. A child who is loved for its own sake takes responsibility for itself first and then for others. Unconditional love does not mean a lack of discipline or training. Its main characteristic is acceptance of a child in its own right, respect for its needs as valid, and recognition of its intrinsic value as a human being.

Diagram A

Images of the Self

Normal Self *(Motivated to please self)*		Hollow Self *(Motivated to please others)*	

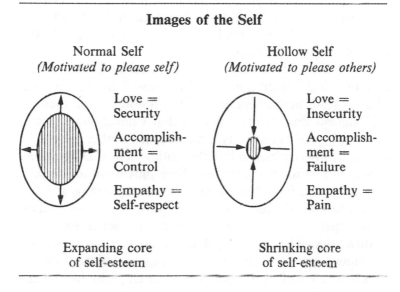

	Love = Security		Love = Insecurity
	Accomplish- ment = Control		Accomplish- ment = Failure
	Empathy = Self-respect		Empathy = Pain

Expanding core of self-esteem	Shrinking core of self-esteem

In theory the cancer-prone person does not receive unconditional love. Neither did I. However, I was not rejected as in the Siegel scenario; I was overprotected and controlled instead. The results are the same. My parents were attentive, loving, and caring, and I had a particularly close relationship with them. My mother was involved with me to an extreme degree, and we established strong identification between us. She lived through me and through my accomplishments. She gained pleasure from my successes as long as they coincided with what she thought was best for me. I gained pleasure, and what I thought was self-esteem, from the special status of being the favorite daughter. I believed that she knew what was best for me because when I did things on my own, in opposition to her advice, they seemed to turn out poorly. I also learned that direct opposition would be met by anger and rejection. Ironically, at the same time she controlled me, she encouraged me to be independent, different, and an achiever. I was all of these things on the surface, and I appeared to be all of these things in the eyes of all who knew me.

The self that I developed appeared to be solid. But the fear of self-disintegration that I expressed in the previous chapter leads me to believe that it was not. I think that my self-concept was always deficient, that I never had a strong sense of myself as an entity independent of other people. In my view, my self looked like the hollow self in Diagram A. It was similar to an egg that has been blown out for decoration purposes. It looked whole, it appeared strong, it functioned to some degree, but it was hollow. Or, more realistically, there was only a tiny core of separateness or authenticity. This core could never grow because accomplishment was converted into a feeling of failure, love for others into a feeling of insecurity, and empathy into pain.

I, like others with a cancer-prone personality, learned early on that it was very important to please my mother, and this model of relationship carried over into my way of relating to the world. Pleasing others therefore became the *major motivation* in my life. My orientation toward others resulted in empathy and sensitivity to the needs of others, but it brought me pain because it was too extreme and unmodulated. As a result I couldn't separate myself from the sorrows of others. I suffered especially when anything bad happened to my sister or my daughters. I also felt unhappy because I was constantly attending to the needs of others while no one was attending to my needs.

Loving also became problematic. The hollow self converts loving into feelings of insecurity. While I was a teenager and a young adult, I did not view my orientation to others as problematic. I understood that my relationship with my mother had its negative aspects, and I knew that I should not live at home after I graduated from college. But I always developed close, loving relationships wherever I went, even if it took me a little time to warm to people. I assumed that all relationships were transient, and I was somewhat insecure about my ability to establish relationships when I entered new social situations. However, at that time, loving was a more positive than negative experience for me.

I believe that the complications began when I married Sy against my parents' wishes. My father was a banker who lived and worked in a prejudiced social milieu. The thought of my marrying someone Jewish made him uncomfortable. What would his colleagues at the bank think? My mother had some of the same negativity about Sy's background, but her main objection was that she believed he would dominate me. At one point I had promised to break off the relationship and for a brief period we dated other people. But the separation was hard for both of us and we decided to get married despite my parents' objections. Predictably, my mother discontinued her relationship with me and, to my surprise, so did the rest of my family. I was angered and hurt by their rejection, but the worst part of it was that I believed that I had handled the situation badly. The experience became a strong verification of my belief that love is conditional and that I should be very careful not to lose Sy's love.

Another characteristic of the hollow self is the inability to turn achievement into a feeling of success. I think that real self-esteem must come from a sequence of wishing for something, determining how to achieve it, working hard to achieve it, deriving pleasure from it or a sense of control of the world, and then allowing one's self to take credit for the effort.

This process is, I suspect, short-circuited in the cancer-prone individual. One works not to satisfy one's own need, but to please someone else, and this makes for great vulnerability. Regardless of how good the effort, or how well the world judges the act, it is a criterion set by the other person not the self that counts. Not only is self-pleasure negated, but more important, there is no gain of control. You are a puppet, and each performance adds to your feeling of helplessness.

The final legacy of the hollow self is the development of negative feelings of all kinds that erode what small sense of self existed. If the desire to please others was my strongest motivation, then fear and insecurity became my most common emotions. My initial fear was of not pleasing my mother. Then my fear turned to concern about not getting good grades, not winning awards, not performing well in any endeavor. Failure became more than not achieving a particular goal—it provoked an emotional crisis. The need to avoid failure at all costs resulted, I believe, in my self-criticism and eventual self-negativity. I think I must have set up extreme criteria for myself as a first line of defense against evaluation by others. If my standards were higher than those around me, then my efforts surely would please the others that I needed to please. The other end of this story is that the fear of doing something wrong made me think always in terms of being wrong.

Another way that I created self-negativity was by redirecting the negativity that I felt to others to myself. I felt frustrated and hostile because I couldn't satisfy my own needs. Since I could not express this hostility to my mother,

I developed unrealistic beliefs about my relationship with her that were self-critical. She was right and I was wrong. Strangely, although I saw my mother as very powerful and always right, I also believed that she was emotionally fragile. I therefore decided I must never make her sad.

I think that the process by which beliefs are accepted that negate the self and excuse the primary caretaker leads to a general lack of moderation and modulation in viewing the world. Thus I developed many exaggerated daydreams that were important to me. I have since learned that such fantasies are common to those with cancer-prone personalities. I imagined that if I were a queen, I would never be alone, and that if I were very rich, I could buy people's affection. At a later point in my life I had a somewhat more modest illusion: If I had a Ph.D., it would gain for me security and independence. Although these dreams gave me comfort, the fact that I took them seriously as standards led to further problems. Since most of my dreams were impossible to achieve, any of my accomplishments in the real world paled in comparison to them. When I obtained my Ph.D. and it did not automatically bring with it any accompanying rewards, my disappointment was terrible.

The quest for the last report card brought out my lack of moderation in setting goals, my inability to accept my achievement as success, and my denial that I was lovable. I hated the self that had been made by and for others. I think it also involved some primitive form of revenge, one final attempt to reverse the hurt and to make my mother sorry for what she had done to me.

Yet the worst terror associated with the last report card was the discovery that my self was hollow, that there was nothing there on which to build. By this time I had dug myself into a groove of automatic reactions that kept me reaffirming my lack of self-worth. My reality became narrower and narrower until there was no way out. Self-esteem became lower and lower, pleasure and satisfaction became nonexistent, and relationships with others became unsatisfactory and distant.

The image of the hollow self that is being eroded by self-negation and self-hatred corresponds well to the cancer that turns on its own cells and destroys them. It is no wonder that the most terrible fear that I glimpsed in my early talks with Sy was not the threat of failure or rejection but the threat of self-disintegration.

4

I Finish My Ph.D. and Become Ill

Although I was afraid for my life on the day that I referred to my upcoming preliminary exam as my last report card, I did not take my intuition seriously. Sy and I were very close to getting at the core problem, the hollow self that had lost the ability to enjoy life. I went on after our talks; the catharsis of our sessions helped to ease the tension for the time being. When I picked up my preliminary exam I knew that I could answer the questions. Full of misguided hubris, I wrote my answers in a lighthearted vein, making jokes, poking fun at some hallowed sociological icons, and enjoying myself a lot. The oral exam started well. In a presession interview one of my professors had praised my paper profusely. But when G. and another member arrived with solemn faces, I knew I was in for trouble. I had obviously incensed them with the casualness of my answers. Even some usually friendly members became very critical. The mood in the group was my undoing. I passed, no question of that, but it was not a brilliant performance.

For a few days I was fine, happy to have the preliminary exam over. Soon, however, the self-critical thoughts began to pour in. In the end I interpreted my performance as a total failure. It was a failure, of course, only in comparison to the superb performance I had hoped for. I almost quit right there and then. I took some time off to gain distance from the experience. In a few weeks I decided that it would be foolish to give up because my data were already in hand and I knew that I could write a dissertation based on them. With a new and very helpful advisor, I finished my Ph.D in November of the following year. My old nemesis, G., was there again at my last oral exam, still critical, still providing me with an excuse to be critical of myself.

So I was finished at last. What did I have now? I had a degree that I felt was a farce. More important, I was left with a sense of failure, not accomplishment. It would have been all right had I been able to accept the degree for its own sake, had I accepted it as a sign that I had succeeded in finishing a difficult task that I had set out to do. That was impossible for me now because, as I proceeded through the program, the stakes had become higher and higher. Good grades, what did they mean? Being awarded a teaching assistantship and even a fellowship meant nothing. I wanted to pass brilliantly, anything else was a failure. So here I was with my degree and, worse still, I had to look for a job.

For a little while I put the idea of future employment out of my mind. It was the end of the year and a time for family celebrations. Thanksgiving came and went, and my life went on in the next month with preparations for Christmas. I remember that it seemed like such an effort to walk around the malls shopping that year. I assumed it was the aftermath of all the hard work I had put into my degree. My tiredness continued, however, after the holidays.

By this time the ground was covered with snow and we now traversed the hiking trail on cross-country skis. Our home is located on forty-five acres of wooded land that abuts hundreds of acres of a state park. We have cut many trails, and the park has made others, providing us with a vast network of walking and skiing trails at our doorstep. An old trolley bed about a mile long is one of our favorite trails because it is perfectly graded and always nicely packed. I began to notice that I could go only a little way on this trail before I was completely fatigued. I used to play a game with myself at this time: I would force myself to take one hundred glides on my skis before I would stop to rest. Every day Sy would be farther and farther ahead of me.

Even more disturbing was the fact that my usual afternoon catnap would often turn into a deep sleep of two or three hours. I attributed these symptoms to recovering from my long ordeal at school. I told myself that I had been in this condition before at times and that it would take me just a little longer to recuperate. I had also developed a disturbing cough a few months before, but that had finally gone away. I believed that I would be fine in time.

Assuming that my physical condition would improve eventually, I began to think about the future. During my many years in school I had dropped all my other activities and I was now becoming bored being home. So I enrolled in a course at the local high school in résumé writing. The week after the course was finished we went to our home at Eastman, New Hampshire, for some skiing. The first actual evidence that something was wrong was that I discovered blood in my urine. A call to my physician at home assured me that it was a common symptom and that I should come in to see him soon but that there was no emergency.

On the second afternoon I remained at home while Sy went cross-country skiing. There was a squirrel running around in the ceiling above me, and it gave me an uncomfortable, eerie feeling. As I lay there shielding my ears from the sound, I suddenly began to feel a pain on my left side near my waist. At first it wasn't so bad, but by the time Sy returned, in an hour, it was intense. This was more severe than the worst pain I had ever experienced. I was confused and frightened. We called to our medical group in Amherst who told us to get there as soon as possible. They also recommended that I take a couple of aspirin or Tylenol. I was told that Dr. Weeks, my regular physician, was not on duty, but that Dr. Chandran, whom I had seen before, would be able to see me.

The trip home, some two and a half hours, was a nightmare. Sy drove at eighty miles an hour while I tried hard to distract myself from the terrible physical discomfort. The miles passed, day turned to night, but the pain did not abate a bit. Then, suddenly, about ten miles from home, it stopped. I arrived pale and exhausted at the doctor's office, where Dr. Chandran was waiting. She took a urine specimen for analysis, examined me, and told me that she believed I had a kidney stone. She told me that no other pain was so intense. I was instructed on how to strain my urine with the hope of catching a stone that might pass naturally. She told me to take a strong painkiller at the first sign of discomfort. The next day it started again, but her remedy worked. I never had another attack.

In the morning Dr. Chandran's office called to report that my urine sample was negative, thus ruling out the possibility of a urinary infection as an alternative to a stone. I was surprised, because by now I was monitoring my temperature and found that it was slightly elevated. I remembered also that I had awakened sweating for the past few weeks, and I was amazed that no infection was found. In my ignorance, these facts were not particularly disturbing. I proceeded to strain my urine, joking that it was like panning for gold. My days as a "prospector" soon ended, however, and the outcome was more unfortunate than not finding gold. When several days passed with no results, my physician took another path. She sent me for a special test to locate the position of the stones if they existed. Instead, they found a growth about the size of a lemon in my left kidney. The bad times had begun.

Dr. Chandran was wonderful when she called with the results, almost apologizing for having to give me such awful news. I remember that day vividly. I suspected that they had found something in my kidney when they had performed the intensive X rays the day before because the doctor had ordered extra pictures to be taken in one particular area. But I was thinking in terms of a kidney stone, nothing more, and my only concern was whether I would have to have an operation. As I put down the phone I became numb. I walked upstairs to tell Sy and then I dressed to go for an immediate appointment with the doctor. I know that I didn't cry, but I don't remember anything else. I moved as if in a dream; some unknown physiological reaction protected me from the full impact of this terrible information. But at some level the information made sense. I had been so tired, so completely exhausted. Now I knew why.

By the time the reality of my situation became manifest to me, there was some good news to soften the blow. The chest X ray that the doctor ordered was negative, indicating that at this point the cancer seemed to be confined to my kidney alone. It was a momentary reprieve, however, because two weeks later, with more tests and an in-depth series of chest X rays, a pulmonary lesion (tumor) was discovered. The only good news was that bone and blood tests showed no other involvement.

It has always been true for me that the many things I worry about never come about, and that the real problems come unexpected like a bolt of lightning. Despite the fact that my mother and grandmother died of cancer, I never believed it would happen to me because I did not take after her family in any way. My mother died of lymphosarcoma, a rather rare and maverick kind of disease that to my knowledge is not hereditary. I did not know at the time what my grandmother's diagnosis was, but I now assume that it was breast cancer, which does run in families. But now it had happened to me, and I had to face the cold reality that my death was imminent.

At this point no one was talking in terms of months or years left for me to live, and we were not asking. I was terribly anemic and weak so I spent long hours in deep sleep. My days were filled with trips to the local hospital for tests and presurgical examinations and with our usual routine of short walks around our pond.

It was hard to look at the beauty of our home and realize that I would not live to see it much longer. I was constantly cold and sad with a dull ache in my chest as I thought about never knowing my grandchildren. Or, I foolishly thought one day, *You are going to die and you will never see what you look like with gray hair.* There were some sweeter thoughts as I pictured my funeral and how sorry my professors would be when they saw what they had done to me. At other times I pictured myself giving away my clothes and my jewelry to my daughters. The afternoons when Sy was at work were hard, but the worst time of all was waking up in the morning. I love to see the new day and at first I would still awaken with a smile. Then in a short few seconds the reality would pour in: *You have cancer and you are going to die.*

As I waited for the day of the operation to come, I had one moment of sheer panic when I trembled with anxiety just before going to bed. I was terrified of the operation because I had never been operated on before. It passed. I never ranted and raved or cried about how unjust the world was or asked why this was happening to me. I knew: I knew that I had gone astray back there so many years ago, and I knew that I must have the operation. We had asked Dr. Weeks, our friend and physician for many years, about a second opinion, but he discouraged us, saying that the surgery was standard and there was no reasonable alternative to it. There was no doubt in my mind either. Now, putting all my symptoms together, including the severe anemia that had been found, I knew that I was close to death. I put myself in the hands of the experts with a sense of resignation, but, at the same time, with the feeling that I still had a lot of fight in me.

My entire family escorted me to the hospital; it was the same local hospital that I had gone to for the birth of my children, and I knew it was an excellent facility with a competent and caring nursing staff. As they wheeled me into the cold, cold operating room a nurse spoke to me by name and asked which kidney they were going to remove. I sat up suddenly and responded, "You mean, you don't know?"

"Yes," she said, rather amused, "we know, but we are supposed to ask you just the same."

"It is my left kidney," I replied, and lay back to rest with a smile on my face. It was a good joke! They removed the kidney along with a few cancerous lymph nodes. I awakened to Sy's words of encouragement that Dr. Miller, my surgeon, believed "he got everything."

Good, I thought, *now to get well.*

My recuperation from the surgery was very rapid. As with so many experiences in my life, the worst fear is in the anticipation; I handle reality very well.

I remained in good spirits during my hospital stay. I thrived on the rest and attention and even enjoyed the food. What I liked the best was that I was never alone. At the end of ten days I was home and ready to go on with the next aspects of my recovery. I no longer dreaded awakening because my mind had adjusted to the presence of my illness. I was happy to have survived the surgery and to be feeling so much better. What I had no way of knowing was that I was entering the most crucial phase of my struggle for life.

The Healing Mind

5

The Interim Period

I returned home from the hospital in excellent spirits. I was recuperating rapidly from the surgery and all of the diagnostic tests done during my stay there were negative. The latest X rays showed that there was still only one lesion on my lung and that it had not changed in size since before the operation. My physicians were in somewhat of a quandary to know how to proceed at this point. In the case of a single lung lesion, surgery would be prescribed. But if the condition of my lung became worse, some other form of therapy would be called for. On the advice of a consultant in Boston, the physicians decided to wait another month before taking the next step, which would be determined by a subsequent X ray. But for the time being I could relax and just think about regaining my strength.

I thrived under the loving care of my family. Sy was a wonderful nurse and housekeeper and had suspended all of his professional activities to tend to me. I knew that he was terribly concerned about me but was careful not to express his concerns for my sake. At unguarded times, however, the depth of his emotions came through. One of those times was when I awakened from surgery to see his loving face and to hear his encouraging words that the surgery was successful. If love could have cured me, I would have been well in that moment. The unspoken reality, however, was that I was still in grave danger.

My general mood now was different from that before the operation. At that time my extreme weakness kept me in a subdued, somewhat dreamy state of mind. The pall of my probable death was like a gray shroud coloring all aspects of my life. There was no terror, just a deep, cold sadness, a constant dull headache, and a slightly sick feeling in the pit of my stomach. The many appointments with physicians filled my days, and I slept long hours at night. In my extra time I concentrated on putting our family finances in order so that Sy would know where to find things in my absence.

The ten days at the hospital, removed from all responsibility except to myself, had been therapeutic for me. I began to gain weight and to feel better than I had in a long time. As my weakness slowly disappeared, the constant sense of my imminent death left me. Of course there were still moments when the seriousness of my situation came pouring in on me, but they happened sporadically. I had many distractions, the most powerful of which was the changing quality of my illness and its variety of physical and psychological demands. Some days were very good days: I had little pain, I read some interesting and amusing books, I walked down the thirty steps to the pond, and I didn't think much about myself and the future. Other days just seemed all wrong: my thoughts would turn to worrying about Lisa, wondering if I would live to see Marty and her new fiancé, Toby, married, and feeling sad that I had never found my path with heart that would engage my energies completely, or that I had never created something of my own.

My major method of dealing with my predicament was to keep busy and to try to keep my mind from myself. I watched television, read, and visited with friends and relatives much more than I ever had. We had never asked about my long-term prognosis and no one had offered any information on it. In the back of my mind I assumed that I would have some time yet to live, and I remained confident that my physicians would be able to remove the single lung tumor by surgery. Although my surgeon had tried to show me the X ray of my lung, I had refused to look at it. I asked only the questions that I needed for the very next step in my medical progress, and I was preparing myself mentally to return to the hospital for another operation. I had a month between X rays in which no new and disturbing news could darken my tenuous equilibrium, and I savored each day.

It was easier on Sy now that I was home and the twice-daily visits to the hospital were over. Now, too, the rest of my family could relieve him more. My daughters, Lisa and Marty, took the first turns at taking care of me, and then my sister came for a week. The household ran very smoothly. It was not always easy for my daughters and my sister, who were used to managing their own households, not to impose their ways on me or on Sy. But they were extremely careful in this respect and in addition rarely lapsed into the petty social interactions that might cause me concern.

On the other hand, we spoke openly about the possible psychological aspects of my illness. I had been aware for some time, even before I became ill, that I fit the general description of the cancer-prone personality. I tended to sacrifice my own needs to the needs of others and to avoid arguments at all costs. Several years before, Sy had been working on a test measuring different components of hostility. I took it for fun, and was not surprised that I got the maximum score on avoidance of expression of anger and hostility. So, in addition to helping me recuperate physically, my family tried to help me mend my ways and become more self-assertive. I agreed with them that I should be more concerned about myself, but the habits of years of living do not change just with advice or with good intentions. It would take a year of therapy (which was to come) to make significant inroads in my old behavior patterns.

The first three weeks of my recovery period went well. My sister, Ruth, was the last of my "live-in nurses," and by the time she left Sy and I had begun to return to our normal life. Every day I felt stronger, taking on my old tasks within limits and with the help of paid homemakers. I started to drive and to walk farther and farther each day. What a thrill it was when I first walked the mile to the top of the trolley road!

Part of my daily regimen was to continue the visualizations that were suggested in the book *Getting Well Again* by Carl Simonton and Stephanie Matthews-Simonton. From the onset of my illness we had all read and reread the classic books on the mind-body connection, especially with respect to the power of visualization to destroy cancer cells. I was convinced that in addition to my lack of assertiveness, my illness was brought on by depression and lack of satisfaction with my life. Sy was very knowledgeable about the latest information on the connection between depression and the immume system. He therefore believed that because my illness had strong psychological factors, I would be a good candidate for renewal by psychological methods. That is, if I could turn around my self-negating way of reacting to the world, my immune system would respond and fight the illness. My conviction on this issue was not as strong as his, but the visualizations made me feel good and the power of his belief was a constant source of hope for me.

From the beginning of my hospitalization I had visualized my cancer disappearing under the onslaught of healthy white blood cells. After sitting quietly for a few moments and trying to relax, I pictured in my mind a scene from a jousting tournament. I would surround a group of cancer cells, black slimy globs of protoplasm, in a jousting ring. The white cells at first were knights on white horses with long lances who would spear one after another of the slimy things. Later the white cells changed into white polar bears who ate the cancer up. The important part of the visualization was that at the end the participants and observers would all yell, "Hip, hip, hurrah . . ." for the job well done. I did the visualization faithfully four times a day as recommended in the book. The times of quiet during the visualization were relaxing for me and gave me a feeling of control. I believed that it was working because I had kept the cancer in my lung in check. Neither Sy nor I saw a need for any other source of psychological support except for our informal discussions at home.

I began to spend the afternoons away from the house because I felt an intense sense of isolation when I was alone there. I went to the exercise salon that I had joined or I shopped, and I began to return to volunteer work on a limited basis for the League of Women Voters. It was time for the annual book drive, and when they called me, as they did every year, I foolishly agreed to price books. This involved not only pricing but a great deal of moving of books from shelves to boxes and back again.

One evening, after I had worked for the League, I developed intense pain along the line of the stitches. We couldn't figure out whether it was from the book-related activity, from overdoing my exercises, or from a talk we had the previous night about my mother. On that occasion I had expressed a great deal of hostility to her for ignoring me when my grandmother was dying and when my sister was born. I recalled my anger and embarrassment on seeing the strange baby who suddenly appeared without warning sucking at my mother's breast.

In order to help me relieve the pain, Sy decided to try a new technique that he had read about, a technique of visualization. He asked me to call up an animal in my imagination that represented the pain. Immediately an image of a golden boa constrictor came to mind: it was wound around my body and putting just enough pressure on me to cause the discomfort that I was feeling. The snake told me that I had no right to intrude in its garden, that I didn't belong there. I, in turn, told the snake that I meant it no harm and asked that it stop hurting me. It retorted that it did not trust me because I was not pure of heart and, like everyone else, I meant to steal its babies for their valuable golden skins.

Despite my denial the serpent did not believe me at all. I begged him to tell me why he thought I was not pure of heart. He replied that I knew the answer and would have to figure it out myself. By now I was physically struggling with the snake, and a feeling of crisis and impasse was developing. I asked if he was hurting me because of my hostility toward my mother and others. The snake hissed out that not expressing hostility had nothing to do with not being pure of heart.

My breathing finally began to quiet down, and the pain abated slightly as I left the realm of fantasy to once more enter the real world. I thought a little and then said that I believed I understood why I was not pure of heart and why the snake held me in its grip. I had gone to the pricing session for the League book sale not to be helpful but to be with other people. I had not really enjoyed myself but had gone to counter the isolation that I felt. This was the sellout then to my fear, just as I had always sold out to my mother's domination so that I wouldn't have to face the fear of her rejection. The golden snake never returned, and the pain never came back quite the same way because I had learned at least to try to be pure of heart.

Sy and I decided to try the same technique to try to understand my intense discomfort at being alone. Visualizing isolation was much more difficult than visualizing pain. After many attempts that we both rejected as trivial, I finally caught the spirit of what I was experiencing. Slowly and with much effort, the vision came. I saw some figures with shrouds—very unclear. Then as they took on a more distinct form, I saw that they were witches standing around a fire. Sy told me to ask them to come over to talk to us. They were frightening to me in the light of the fire, but they were more horrible as they came closer. They laughed at me and started to poke at me with their sticks. The visualization was so real and their presence was so chilling to me that I burst into tears over the interaction with them.

Sy told me to ask them what I could do to get rid of the awful fear of isolation. Finally they revealed their price: It was that I make a sacrifice so that they could become beautiful and mingle with other people. When I heard their price I began to tremble. In an almost inaudible voice I whispered, "They want my children so they can turn them into witches like them, but I'll never do it. I'll never give them my children!"

Sy then told me to destroy them, but I told him that I couldn't possibly do it. He urged me to try to turn my fear to wrath, to try to imagine a creature that could help me. The image that came to me was a white winged horse. He told me to mount the horse and to supply myself with a weapon that would destroy them. I refused to kill them myself, but said that the wings of the horse would fan the flames of their fire, which would turn back on them and destroy them.

There was only one problem with this scenario—the horse and I were one now and I couldn't get airborne. The wings were so heavy that I couldn't flap them hard enough to catch the breeze. The harder I tried, the more I failed and the more the witches laughed at me. Sy joined my fantasy for real when he told me that another horse who loved the first horse very much would join her and together they would destroy the witches. The other horse flew above me and made a vacuum into which I could take off. Once in the air, I flew effortlessly and fanned the fire into a huge blaze. The witches ran here and there trying to avoid the flames, but in the end they were consumed by the fire.

I practiced the scene over and over again until it became easy, but I never enjoyed it. I liked to fly, but I felt sorry for the witches, no matter how mean they were to me. Sy felt that it was a mistake to feel sympathy for them because they would take advantage of any mercy that I displayed. He felt that they would use any deception and illusion they could to control me. I was not so sure but I did agree with him that I must assume the right to soar into the world and be free of their influence.

After the session we discussed the meaning of the images. Although I had begun with the concept of isolation in mind, I knew that the witches related to my mother, particularly the way she would poke at me and shame me. They probably represented my fear of isolation if I did not acquiesce to her demands. Sy added that in destroying the witches I was only destroying the hostile parts of our relationship, the witch part of it, and leaving the loving part intact. This was necessary for me to be free, autonomous, and not ensnared by fear and abandonment.

The concept that I had a great deal of conflict between the need for association and the need for autonomy was not new. I believed I had to buy affection and that no one would love me if I were myself, i.e., if I attended to my own wants. I knew also that I felt that I had to carry the burden of being responsible for my mother's well-being, that she would die at some level if I broke the bond with her. In fact, my mother died of cancer within four years of my break with the family when I married Sy. Luckily, she and I were reconciled before she died. However, the model that females in our family died after the loss of a child (my grandmother at the death of Teddy, my mother at the break with me) was reinforced by the timing of my mother's death.

The two imagery sessions that I described above were our first attempts at using my imagination to alleviate difficult feelings and moods. But although we were dealing with the essential aspects of visualization, we had not found the most effective way to use them for my integration. The other thing that we were unaware of was that powerful forces were at work in my larger environment to undermine what progress we were making.

In the weeks that followed two personal interactions occurred that resulted in extended periods of depression for me. The first incident involved the death of a close relative of mine. Her will was settled shortly after I left the hospital. When I discovered that I had been left a smaller portion than my sister or my four cousins, I took it as a personal rejection and brooded for weeks about how I had alienated my relative. The second incident involved an argument with my sister over the telephone that left me confused and very hurt. The most important aspect of these interactions was that they highlighted my inability to express justifiable anger at those who had hurt me. These incidents made it clear that my self-negating personality was still intact, could color my view of the world, and resulted in psychologically induced stress and physical pain.

Before long it was time for me to go to the hospital for the X ray to see what was happening with my lung. I knew that I wouldn't get the results until the day after, when I had an appointment with the oncologist who was taking over my case. So, after returning from the hospital, I tried to relax for the rest of the day.

I was surprised on the afternoon of the X ray by a call from Will Weeks, our original physician, who told me that my case was to be presented the next day at the hospital because of its unique circumstances and the question of whether to operate or not. I told him about my wellness visualizations, which I was sure had held the disease to the one spot. He is a very religious man who believes in miracles and the power of prayer so he wanted to tell the assembled physicians about the Simonton method of visualizing the cancer disappearing. I gave him the information and put the whole thing out of my mind.

Tuesday, April 23, 1985, dawned as a beautiful day. My appointment was for early afternoon and Sy was taking me. It was about noon. We were dressing to go when I heard a car pull up to the front driveway. I looked out of the window and saw Dr. Weeks walking up the path. I couldn't figure out what he was doing here, but something told me that it was not a good sign. Somehow it felt strange and ominous. As he walked into the room he burst into a rapid flow of words—something about the fact that we were his friends and he wanted us to hear the news from him. It seemed that during the presentation he told the group that there was a new X ray that would be of interest and would give them the final disposition to the case.

When the pictures were shown on the screen at the hospital, they all could see that the lung lesion was discernibly bigger than it had been a month before and there now was a second lesion below the first. Case closed! No operation advised. Prognosis, very grim. He told us to ask the oncologist to be very frank with us about possible next steps. We got the impression that he didn't have much confidence in the therapeutic benefits of chemotherapy for my case and said that if it were he, he might decide to do nothing. He left as quickly as he came and left us in a state of complete upheaval.

I sat down at the dining-room table to steady my weakening legs. I put my head in my hands and just sat trying to absorb what had just happened. I didn't cry, but I just kept shaking my head. I didn't understand. How could this be? I felt so well, and there was no indication whatever that I was getting worse. And yet the news was undeniable. Sy took me in his arms and held me, and then I cried to let out the tension. We continued to dress in silence and then got into the car. The oncologist's office was at least a half hour away and we had never been there before so we started early. In truth, neither of us could think of anything else to do.

The oncologist spent over a half hour talking to us. He seemed relieved when we told him that we already knew about the newest X ray. He methodically reviewed my case: tumor in the kidney, some spreading to the lymph nodes in the primary area, single lung tumor, and now enlarged tumor and another just below. We discussed chemotherapy, but like Dr. Weeks he told us that it was not effective for this kind of cancer. Surgery was the only acceptable treatment, and that now was not possible. Sy then asked him about psychological cures and about the possibility of remission. His response was impatient and somewhat annoyed. He said that he did not approve of Simonton's book and that if we wanted to pursue quack remedies, he would not encourage us.

Finally we came to the ultimate question, the one that he did not want us to ask and the one that I did not want him to answer. Sy asked, "How much longer does Alice have?"

He hesitated, and then reluctantly responded. "Well, in cases like this, where the cancer has spread in the lung and is probably growing in the primary area as well, I'd say about three months."

I gasped for air as I heard his reply, and I kept saying over and over to myself, "So this is what it is to be. This is what it is to be. Oh, no!" I brought my hand to my mouth to stifle a cry and grit my teeth to keep from sobbing. I couldn't look at the doctor at all. But I did see Sy. His face had turned white.

The doctor continued to talk. "Although we have no standard treatment to offer you, I've been in touch with physicians at Boston who can offer you an experimental interferon treatment. It might extend your time for a few months. If I were you, that's where I would go."

He gave us the telephone number and said that he would arrange for me to pick up my records. His nurse came in at that moment and he left the room. It seemed clear to us that the interview was over. We left his office with little hope, especially on my part. But Sy would not give up, and he was already planning the strategy that was to lead to my eventual recovery.

6

We Mobilize

The two days that followed the visit to the oncologist's office were the most distressing ones I experienced. I felt that a black box had slammed down on me, completely obstructing my view and restricting my movements. I wanted to crawl into a corner and never come out. I pictured what it would be like to be dead, and I was filled with terror at what I saw. All of the hopelessness and helplessness that I had nurtured during the past years took over my personality. I could see no way out.

I remember walking around the pond with Sy on the next afternoon. With tears in my eyes, I told him that everyone might be better off if I were dead. I had messed up the children's lives by overprotecting them and I regretted that. And he—well he might be better off with a younger wife, a newer model, who could keep up with him. He stopped and, without words, took me in his arms and held me tightly. "I don't want any other model," he said. "I just want you to get well, and we are going to do everything in our power to make that happen."

There were other ways in which this was a hard time for me. Added to the depressing news about my condition was the disappointment in the process of visualization. I had faithfully done my anticancer images at least four times a day. I had had such confidence in the method, and now I had nothing.

But while I was completely dejected for the first time, my family came alive with vitality. Sy now absolutely insisted that I should have an independent therapist so he called several of our friends who have private practices in Amherst for recommendations. The day after I saw the oncologist I went for my first therapy session with a lovely person who was very easy to talk to. We talked about death and about why I was afraid to die. It turned out that there were too many unfinished areas in my life, too much that I wanted for my children that I thought they needed me for. We talked about letting go. It made sense preparing for the inevitable, but I knew that for a real fight for my life, I needed someone else.

Lisa, in the meanwhile, had been asking for advice about therapists among her friends in New York and Boston. Whenever she said that we needed someone in the Amherst area, the name of Dorothy Firman came up. Lisa had told Sy about this several weeks before, but he was reluctant because the therapist's training was in a type of therapy that was unknown to him and he was afraid that it was an unorthodox kind of treatment.

The following weekend the whole family was gathered in Amherst for my birthday. While shopping downtown Lisa and Sy passed the Synthesis Center, where Dorothy Firman worked, and Lisa again insisted that she wanted me to try it out. So Sy called for an appointment for me for the following week. That was not all we were to do, however. We found Dr. Rechtschaffen, a holistic physician, who advised me on a sound nutritional approach to cancer, and Peggy Roggenbuck, a therapist trained in the Simonton method, who checked out my visualization. We also decided to make an appointment with the Simonton Cancer Institute so that

I could have the benefit of direct contact with Simonton himself.

Lisa did more for me than find me a therapist. She sat me down and told me that she had written an affirmation for me that she would explain and that she wanted me to follow. I had never heard of the concept of affirmation before, but I listened carefully as she explained that she believed there were profound connections between the spoken word and the material world, and that I was to be meticulous with what entered my mind and my language, always projecting health and a favorable outcome. She composed an affirmation that I was to repeat every time I meditated. It read as follows:

My Affirmation

I am connected to my deepest wisdom and guidance.

All I need for perfect and total healing is coming to me naturally and effortlessly.

I am guided in every phase of this healing.

I am finding all I need for every aspect of the healing, on every level: physical, emotional, mental, and spiritual.

This includes perfect physicians, nutritionists, healers, advisors, programs, and information.

All the information and all of my decisions are made for my highest good and are perfectly aligned with my affirmation and are energizing of:
perfect health
wholeness
and
balance.
Thank you for this guidance and understanding.

I found great comfort in these words whenever I repeated them. But the amazing thing was that within a week the first part of the affirmation came true.

On the following Monday, Sy and I had our first session with Dorothy Firman, who asked me to call her Didi. We met in the Synthesis Center, a small, homey building in town. Didi was informally dressed and we all sat on low cushions in the main room of the center. I was impressed by her warmth, her professionalism, and her quiet confidence. Sy began by telling her that our job was to turn me around psychologically in a very short period of time so that my immune system would react to fight the cancer. Quite a tall order! Didi much later admitted to me that she was terrified by the enormous task we wished her to undertake, but she was compelled by the challenge and by Sy's determination. Her first question to both of us was, "Why didn't Alice call me instead of you, Sy?" Her next comment was that she wanted to hear from me now. I remember very little about that first meeting except that we decided to meet in her home, which was not far from where Sy and I live.

We were heartened by our interview with Didi. Sy and she established an immediate rapport when they learned that their professional views were compatible. She told Sy that she had heard his talk at a recent conference at Amherst College featuring the Dalai Lama and other scholars interested in forging an integration between Eastern and Western psychology. Sy had been asked to present his theory of personality because it emphasizes the way people automatically construct a view of reality. There were differences between them too: Didi's orientation, we learned, was spiritual and intuitive, while Sy's was more rational. The connecting link was that Sy was attempting to express the kinds of esoteric concepts endorsed by Didi in scientific terms. The common thread shared by Didi and Sy was very important in my eventual recovery. They acted as independent but complementary therapists in a unique team approach to therapy.

The other change that we made was to drop the services of the oncologist, whose office was some distance from our home, in favor of our family physician and friend, Dr. Weeks. It was Dr. Weeks who later handled all of my references to our Health Maintenance Organization (HMO), where he was on the staff. We learned that the cost of the diagnostic visit to the Boston clinic would be covered by the HMO and we would make decisions about paying for the actual treatment as we went along. I was very satisfied with this arrangement.

By this time our friends and casual acquaintances were also involved in a search for alternative approaches to healing. Through Lynn Robinson and her connection with the Interface Center in Boston, we heard about Bernie Siegel. Lynn sent me some tapes that he had recorded in Boston that I found very helpful. I responded immediately to his wonderful sense of humor, and was encouraged by his stories of "exceptional patients" who had beaten cancer. At that time he was known locally as a surgeon who encouraged his patients to meditate and to try to contact their inner healing potential. Now, with the publication of *Love, Medicine, and Miracles,* he has a national reputation. By chance he was conducting a weekend retreat at the Rowe Conference Center nearby, and we drove up to hear the introductory lecture. Had we not already begun with Didi, I am sure I would have joined the group sessions that Dr. Siegel conducted in New Haven. But for the present we decided to continue with the program that we had set up locally.

Another alternative treatment that we learned about was one that was being conducted at the Livingston–Wheeler

Medical Clinic in San Diego. I spoke to a woman who said that their immunotherapy program had helped her considerably. We bought Dr. Wheeler's book, *The Conquest of Cancer: Vaccines and Diet,* which described the clinic, but considered this as a last resort. We learned also that the mother of a friend of a friend of Lisa had been successful in holding her kidney cancer in remission with a self-inoculation process done by a hospital in Albany. This was impossible for me because it required a piece of the cancerous material, but again we stored the information for future reference. The important thing about each of these contacts was that we knew that other possibilities existed and this helped to allay our previous sense of helplessness.

The broader family unit, consisting of Sy's nephews and niece, gave me tremendous support and advice, which came out of theoretical and spiritual backgrounds that were new to me. Stewart, Sy's brother Bunny's youngest son, had been meditating for years and often had spoken to us about the Self-Realization Fellowship (SRF) based in California. He had left the little paperback called the *Autobiography of a Yogi,* by Parmahansa Yogananda, for us to read. I had never read it. After some conversations with Stew on the telephone, I realized that both he and his fiancée, Julie, were intensely religious people. I found that I could relate to many of their ideas. Although the SRF was based on the teaching of a Hindu saint, it accepted Christ as one of many holy men that it venerated. Devotees go through a long period of training in the meditation techniques taught by Yogananda; Stew had completed his training years before, but Julie had been in the process of learning when she had stayed with us several months before. All this prepared me to learn from Stew and from the wisdom of these teachings. I could not anticipate, however, how close our relationship would become and how important it would be in my recovery.

Within a few weeks of hearing of my illness, Stew wrote a letter outlining what he believed to be the essence of my psychological problems. I must admit that I opened the first letter with much trepidation, fearful of what strange things it would contain. I was in tears, however, when I finally read it. It began with a beautiful statement of how much I had always meant to him as a child, how much he had enjoyed his stays with us, and how much he had enjoyed the giving atmosphere of our home. I was touched and impressed with his analysis. The essential message was to forgive myself and turn the love that I had given to others on myself for healing.

This advice was not the only thing that Stew gave me: he encouraged me to read, and he slowly introduced me to his concept of God. First, I finished the *Autobiography of a Yogi,* the delightful story of the guru's boyhood in India, his training as a swami, and his eventual journey to the West to teach his doctrine of Hinduism and Christianity. From these I went on to read his book *Scientific Healing Affirmations.* Prepared now for its message by Lisa's affirmation lecture, I began to understand the task before me. Yogananda said, "Appeal to that Power [God] with infinite confidence, casting out all doubt." But he warned that once the seed is sown, "Do not pluck it frequently to see whether it has germinated." And, remember, "Patient and attentive repetition are wonder workers."

Submission to the cosmic will was stressed and this concept was particularly comforting to me. I remembered that Bernie Siegel had told the story of one patient who had recovered from cancer by "leaving her troubles to God." Sometimes in periods when I felt particularly helpless, it would make me feel better to just repeat over and over, "I submit myself to the will of God; I submit myself to the will of God." The word *God* had no particular meaning to me; I said it by rote as a child would repeat a prayer. In another sense, as time went on and I meditated more and more, Stew's concept of "knowing God" through meditation became easier for me to understand and accept. In this light I understood what Yogananda meant when he said, "Prayers should be used not to beg for transitory favors, but to enable man to reclaim the divine treasure that in his ignorance he had thought lost." God, in this way, was some sort of cosmic being much too complicated to even define and much too overwhelming to understand except on an intuitive level. This was easy for me because my concept of God had always been amorphous at best.

Anna, Stew's sister, introduced me to another spiritual approach. Anna had attended many lectures and workshops on psychological self-healing. In an early letter she wrote that she felt that her education had been lacking in lessons of the spirit. So, as a young woman, she had taken this task on herself. She wrote, "There is an energy which I don't understand but am very aware of. It is transcendent and greater than each of us. What I've learned is that it can be called on for help, and if we relax into it, and let it work, anything can happen. It does the work, if we step aside, in love, and simply let it. It may not seem logical, but it sure is powerful."

She went on to say that her favorite teacher is Eric Butterworth, whose tape on visualizing oneself in light she was sending me. She ended by saying that she hoped that I would not be turned off by the allusions to God and Jesus but would take the best part of the tape to heart and ignore the rest. I listened to the tape with the "light" meditation often and included it in my regular meditation routine. I have been told that some people find it impossible to imagine themselves in this way, but it was easy for me and very successful in inducing a feeling of well-being and power.

The various kinds of advice I received reinforced each other. The approaches also fit well with my religious beliefs, simple as they were. I incorporated them all into my assault on my sickness. Despite my initial disappointment, I never gave up on the Simonton method of visualization. In fact, I became more devoted to it than ever, urged on by Sy, who said that it was indeed possible to be cured.

Once the first part of my affirmation was in place, we were able to turn to the experimental physical therapy suggested by the oncologist. I made an appointment with the Dana Farber Cancer Clinic in Boston to talk about their interferon program. That was a hard trip. The most difficult part for me was looking at the ominous chest X ray for the first time. Being able to face the reality of the tumors in my lung was a part of the new approach to my illness—I was engaging it now, not running away from it. The hospital and all of the staff were wonderful. I was given a complete examination and then they talked to me about the program for over an hour.

First they told me that the prognosis by my oncologist might be somewhat exaggerated. They made no specific promises, but they certainly gave me a longer time frame than I had before speaking to them. This was good news. They also brought up the "myth" that sometimes this type of cancer healed itself after the removal of the primary site. Sy was immediately interested in what they had to say. "What are you talking about?" he asked.

"Well," the chief physician responded, "general practitioners have the impression that in rare cases remission of kidney cancer occurs after the removal of the diseased kidney. We have been working with this particular kind of can-

cer for years and have never seen evidence of such a phe-
nomenon, but somehow the idea persists."

Sy then told them about the psychological work that we
had been doing and of his belief that a psychological change
might induce a change in the immune system. Although
they were not negative or critical of what Sy was saying,
they completely denied the possibility of a psychological
cure. They told us that if it made us feel good to believe it
would help, they had no objection to it as long as it did not
prevent us from seeking appropriate medical treatment.

They turned the conversation to the details of their new
program. They were particularly excited about the gamma
interferon that they were trying because they were reporting
a positive reaction rate in 40 percent of their patients. One
person actually was able to be off the program completely,
while others had shown great improvement. This was much
more promising than any other chemical treatment, which
they said never went beyond 10 percent. We were impressed.

Then came the bad news about the details of the treatment. It comprised a two- to three-week hospitalization period in which I would experience very severe, flu-like symptoms. Then, if there was improvement—at least 50 percent
reduction in the lesion—I would have to receive injections
three times a week, every other week, *forever.* I was stunned!
The idea of such chemical dependency was appalling to me;
I seriously wondered what it would do to our lives.

When I asked about the cost it turned out to be stagger-
ing—from $30,000 to $40,000 a year. They said that some
patients were covered by health insurance, but coverage was
not guaranteed because of the status of the program as
experimental. They told us that some families rented an
apartment in Boston; others came from hours away for their
injections. It sounded like a nightmare to me, but I agreed

to take the rest of the tests required to prepare me for the program in case I decided to go along with it.

After the physicians left we remained with the program director, who urged me to join. She said that I was an excellent candidate and she couldn't understand my reluctance. Then, when my hesitance continued, she turned to me and said emphatically, "You're going to die of this illness you know, eventually!" "Yes," I said, "I know that." But in my heart I told myself that I still had the choice of how I would die.

The drive home was not good. Sy, too, was annoyed with me for always looking at the dark side of things. I felt acutely depressed. We had a few weeks to decide about the interferon program, but we were also impressed with the fact that it would not be available forever. Each program was limited to a given number of cases, and when that number was reached the program was closed. In Boston they were now entering the thirtieth or so case out of about forty-five. The most important aspect of the trip to Boston was that we now knew what this alternative would mean.

I was becoming mobilized and ready to fight for my life. At the same time I knew that I had to be prepared to die, that this was a real possibility. So I stopped looking for ways to distract myself and I put myself on a strict schedule of meditation and therapy. Nothing was allowed to interrupt my meditation times, which were early in the morning before breakfast, at noon, at sunset, and before going to bed.

My meditation began with a few minutes of quiet in which I tensed and then relaxed each part of my body, beginning with my head. Soon I began my Vipassana meditation, which simply involves attending to the breath. I could feel the intake and outtake of breath in my nostrils. If some inner or outside sound took me away from my task, I would note what the stimulus was and try to let it go. When I had achieved a certain concentration level I began my visualization of killing the cancer cells. I enjoyed destroying the black globs in my first visualization, either by piercing them with spears or by eating them up. When I could see that the pile of cancer cells had diminished, I changed to another image. I then tried to view myself in light. Sometimes I was very successful in this endeavor and sometimes I could not hold the image for more than a few seconds. I ended as I began, with watching my breath. The whole process took at least forty-five minutes and often longer.

Before long the effect of this regimen began to take effect and, for the most part, I was calm.

Strangely and wonderfully, time itself began to slow down: days became like weeks, and weeks were like months. When I would tell people about it they always asked, "Is that good?" and I would reply, "Oh, yes, it is very good that time is slowing down for me, because I have so little time."

I continued to read everything that I could get my hands on about healing. Lisa sent me an article about a man with AIDS who had taken interferon treatments and then had decided to try a multifaceted approach similar to mine. As with me, he was supported by the love of a significant other who was deeply devoted to him. Amazingly, he succeeded. There were other cases too. An investigative reporter named Judith Glassman interviewed a group of cancer survivors, all of whom had some sort of physical therapy that they believed in very much, a devoted friend, and a very strong fighting spirit. Again, all of these things were helpful because they gave me hope.

Lisa also sent me a reprint from a book by David Spangler called *The Laws of Manifestation*. I knew that Spangler was one of the founders of Findhorn, a spiritual community in Scotland that emphasizes the cooperation between humanity and nature. However, I had never read any of his writings. In her note to me Lisa admitted that the reading was a little dense, but to help simplify matters she had underlined certain sections for my special attention.

There were several basic principles of manifestation outlined in the article. The first point was that it was a natural process that would turn energy from one level of reality to another. Second, in order for manifestation to work, Spangler said we must believe that what is to be manifested already exists. Third, the manifestation process requires faith. Spangler quoted the New Testament definition of faith, from Hebrews 11:1: "Faith is the substance of things hoped for, the evidence of things unseen." Faith gives substance to our hopes and makes us certain of realities we do not see. The fourth principle was that manifestation is the process of releasing a potential. An example would be my affirmation of releasing myself into perfect health.

So far these ideas were somewhat clear. Moreover, it made sense to me that emotional energy is the fuel for manifestation for good or bad. That is, worry is as potent as faith, only in the opposite direction. But what I had to read over and over again without really understanding was the part about faith and hope. Spangler says that faith is different from hope. Faith involves *knowing* and is consequently powerful. Hope, on the other hand, involves *not knowing:* it is not single-pointed and it admits fear that the manifestation might not work. Hope, therefore, is a lack of unity and dissipates energy; faith, by contrast, is one-pointed *knowing.*

The part about will was equally difficult for me to understand. Of this Spangler said, "Will creates through revelation of what is the nature of the Source and the Center, the ultimate authority. Rather than acting as a pressure upon the surface of things, it acts as a magnet drawing the comparable divine nature from out of the heart of things."

All of this was strange to me. How can faith be based on knowing? It seemed to me that one has faith about things that one *doesn't* know, or else one would not need faith. How could will not involve acting on things? That was contrary to my experience and my intuition. When I thought about my will I saw myself as persistent, nose to the grindstone, or, as now, keeping strictly to my meditation schedule.

The Spangler article didn't make sense to me, but I kept on reading because I could understand his idea of letting go. From three or four sources I had learned that letting go was important. Lisa had said it, Anna felt that you had to let something happen, and Stew and Yogananda talked about working but not watching too closely for results. I kept reading, meditating, visualizing, and being slowly transported into a state of altered consciousness from which came increased understanding.

It happened in little steps, this process of understanding. Sy kept after me to meet with him every evening, to keep up my meditation, and to not lapse into a state of helplessness; that he feared the most of all. If in an emotional state I would avow that I wanted to live, he would counter with, "Why, tell me why?" At first I could only say that I wanted very much to grow old with him. It became a little joke with us. Or that I wanted to see my daughters married or to see my grandchildren. But he would not accept these answers. He wanted me to have a motivation of my own. It was a while in coming, just like my understanding of manifestation and faith, but come it did.

There were occasional dramatic events that let me know I was on the right track. One evening, after our trip to Boston, I couldn't sleep and got up to meditate. At this point I was doing my polar-bear-eating-the-bad-cancer-cells visualization, repeating my affirmation and picturing myself in light. After that I would concentrate attention on my breath. I was angry with Sy for being critical of my attitude following our trip to the Dana Farber Clinic. At the same time I knew that he was my most important support and the person that I loved most dearly. I can't remember how the thought started, but an image of going away came to mind and became increasingly strong. I let it take me where it would and suddenly the idea came to mind that despite my love for Sy, if it meant leaving him in order to get better, I would do it. In other words, if my life were on the line in a decision between relating and living, I would choose to live. It was a very important insight, because in the past I had always made the opposite decision. The knowledge that it would be different now was a source of great strength to me. I kept that knowledge with me and discussed it with Didi. I believe that this assurance to myself that at last I could let my life come first was the beginning of the motivation that I needed to live. Finally, I wanted to live just for me.

Although at the time I felt that Sy had dragged me into therapy at a rather low point of my illness, in retrospect I was quite well prepared. We had all of my helping facilities in place: the physicians, the diet, the review of my visualizations, and the beginning of a spiritual awakening. I felt very well physically. Although the surgical wound was not completely healed and bothered me when I became tired, there was nothing else wrong with me that I could detect. In addition, I was determined to change the way that I related to the world.

By the beginning of May, just two weeks after we had learned about my worsening condition, the family entered a period of relative calm in which each one of us understood the role that we were to play. We knew that we had done all that we could, and we just had to wait to see if results would be forthcoming.

7

My Two Therapists

How does one begin in therapy? Not at the beginning—I was born, et cetera. At the heart of the pain? The story of the Ph.D? No, not that either. We began with a vision, a tiny goal that we knew we could achieve. Didi told me that she had read the Simonton book and she was impressed with one fact: His patients did not always live, but they all extended their lives beyond the medical expectancy for their case and enhanced its quality. She asked me to pick a time, not so far away in the future, that I wanted to strive for. I thought awhile. It was now spring. I had met with the oncologist on April 23, and by his estimate I could not live beyond the end of July. I could do better than that! So I opted for December. I told her that I wanted to live to see the first snow. I love the winter; another winter would be what I would aim for.

In the very first days I did not keep notes or a diary, so I can't give specific details about my introduction to the method of psychosynthesis. What I can do is to describe some of its general principles. They are taken from a pamphlet entitled *Psychosynthesis: Conscious Evolution,* which Didi gave me in those early days.

In essence the theory assumes that evolution or synthesis is a natural process of growth toward wholeness, integration, and our deepest and highest self. That is, a person is more than his/her neuroses, fantasies, conflicts, or symptoms; a person is more than self. There is a transpersonal dimension to a human being: it can be thought of as the higher self, the true self, the spiritual, or the Hindu life principle called the atman. This higher self is a permanent aspect of psychic experience that is the link to the universal. It is also our inner guide, the part of us with a sense of purpose for the life of the person.

The process of therapy (synthesis) is more important than the content of the therapy or the outcome. The client's inner wisdom and sense of rightness dictate how that process is best facilitated or accessed by the guide. The power of the therapy is in the energy of the higher self of the client, not in the therapist. The personal self is the pure center of the personality, a center of consciousness and will. When aligned with the higher self the personal self can become available as the directing and harmonizing agent of the personality in the world. Unconditional love is the cornerstone of transpersonal therapy.

It feels strange to read these statements over now. All that I remember being emphasized was the growth toward wholeness, the fact that the process was more important than the goal, and the importance of learning to be strong in the world. I also remember an early discussion of spirituality. Didi asked what my spiritual inclinations were, and I told her that I had none. I consider myself to be a Protestant, but formal religion has never appealed to me.

I told her, also, that both Sy and I had learned Vipassana "insight" meditation at Barre, Massachusetts, and that we had been meditating for several years. I found that the meditation practice made it easy for me to do the cancer-destroying visualizations because I was used to sitting quietly and focusing my attention on inner processes. I was grateful for this advanced preparation. Didi made a mental note of it all and we moved on.

We moved on very quickly because we knew that we might not have much time. Immediately we attacked the core problem of my relationship to my mother. Didi had given me a pamphlet that she and her mother, Julie Firman, had written called *Mothers and Daughters.* They used it to conduct workshops on mother-daughter relations. I read it before our first therapy session and went with the exercises filled out. It led to an immediate breakthrough.

I went into the first therapy session with two pictures that I had drawn according to the instructions in the pamphlet. One was of me as a three-year-old dancing in a pink tutu with my mother standing by looking very pleased. The story I told to the picture is: "My mother is happy to see that I'm going to do a solo in the recital. But my feeling is that I don't like the fact that she makes me lie about my age at dancing school. When I complain she tells me that everybody does it."

The second picture, of my mother and me in later years, was very different from the first one. Here, in stick figures and drab colors, was my mother in a dark shroud reaching out for me while I ran away. The story line is brief: "My mother is reaching out to me to pull me into the grave with her and I am terrified."

Didi asked me if I would be willing to visualize this scene. Although I was uncomfortable about trying this technique for the first time, I agreed. She immediately put me at ease. After sitting quietly for a few moments she asked me to picture in my mind the scene that I had drawn. As soon as the image appeared my mother's image moved toward me and tried to pull me into a nearby grave. I was filled with terror; my heart began to beat rapidly and my breath came in gasps. I tried to resist with all my might. Didi guided me through the visualization and insisted that I tell my mother that I would not go with her. "I will not go," I screamed. "I WILL NOT GO!" Over and over again I shouted it, until I began to believe it myself. After the session was over I was exhausted by the intensity of the emotional experience.

When I told Sy about the therapy sessions he expressed concern about possible negative effects of the emotional catharsis that I was experiencing. As a therapist himself, he knew that sometimes symptoms get worse before they get better, and he warned that some of these intense visualizations might have temporary negative ramifications. He didn't tell me not to do the visualizations with Didi, but he wanted me to be forewarned.

It is strange that as fearful as I am in general, I never took his concerns seriously. Perhaps it was because intuitively I knew that I had nothing to fear, or I felt that I had nothing to lose, or because intellectually I could see how well the method of visualization worked for me. My early work with Sy had taught me that it took me immediately to the emotional core of the issues that were disturbing me. Now, under Didi's tutorship, I learned that the process of guided visualization actually reduced the intensity of the fears, hostility, or other emotions I was feeling.

The first evidence that the therapy was working was that within a week the deep feelings of resentment for my mother began to change. In its place I developed a strong feeling of love for her and a sense that I could tap her love in my struggle to get well. I assume that as I asserted myself against her in my mind, I allowed myself to forgive her in my heart. I am also sure that this dramatic progress was facilitated by the preliminary work that Sy and I had done on the same subject.

Although the change in my feelings about my mother seemed to take place very rapidly, the actual process took the next few weeks to accomplish. Didi and I spent several more sessions discussing the specifics of the mother-daughter relationship. Through the exercises in the little booklet I came to realize how similar my mother and I are: we are both intuitive, smart, open, warm, loving, and dominant, but in different ways. We did exercises of forgiveness with my mother too. Once the threshold of the dark death visualization had been passed, Didi stressed the love that was between my mother and me.

We talked some more about the demand that I had to have a perfect mother, one who should give me everlasting, unconditional love. Didi spoke frankly about the fact that I must discontinue such expectations, that no such relationship could exist with another person, even one's mother. She told me that she had once searched the world over for the perfect guru, always to be disappointed. Finally she had a dream in which she was told that this would be the last time she would ever dream of this quest and it was time to give it up.

I don't know how, but these talks eventually sank in too. I also learned to not talk about the "last" step of any process; I learned to think about life as a journey, not the end. My old desires died hard, but in time they did fade. Even now, if I hear myself lapsing into my old ways of thinking, I just smile to myself and let them go

Although at the time it was the visualizations themselves and the reduced emotionality that stood out, I realize that the training in dealing with the situations *within the visualization* was probably more important. By making me tell my mother that I would not go with her, Didi was training me to be assertive. The training began within the visualizations, which were completely under my control. Later we applied the same methods to real people and situations in the real world.

I worked very hard at my twice-weekly sessions with Didi. I read everything she gave me and tried to do the other assignments as well. But the time between sessions were productive too. Sy and I continued to talk almost every evening. At his instigation we talked about whatever was bothering me at the time. In essence I had two therapists, different but complementary. With Didi I was emotional; I was beginning to learn to use my intuition and to train my will. With Sy I was taking an eclectic, psychodynamic approach. Especially in the later phases of therapy, Sy and I both summarized rationally what had occurred with Didi and planned my next steps. Sy and I did a lot of debriefing.

In the initial phases of therapy, however, we often worked in depth on the same issues that I was working on with Didi. In regard to my attitude toward my mother, we began with the concern about whether I should express or avoid hostility. Sy's initial thought was that expression might exacerbate guilt reactions, which might in turn cause the disease to get worse. At my insistence we took a direct frontal attack on the problem via more fantasy.

I started by asking for help in answering the question about expressing hostility; I waited to see what would come to mind. An elephant appeared in my thoughts, and, as always, once the first image appeared, a story line followed. The elephant lifted me onto his back. The sensation of being so high made me dizzy, but it gave me a new perspective from which to view the everyday life of the village in which the elephant lived. Specifically, I could not see the scowls on people's faces as they looked at me. Just experiencing this image made me realize that the solution to my anger was to view things from a higher perspective. This exercise helped me not only to forgive my mother but to relate better to Sy emotionally. It was a freeing experience for me in many ways.

A day later, in another evening session, Sy read to me a summary of the stories I had told to the Thematic Apperception Test (TAT) many years ago when we both were students in Wisconsin. Sy had needed twenty or so subjects for his course on the TAT and I had volunteered. Recently he had extracted from my responses nine beliefs, most of which seemed very maladaptive. He thought it might help me to get rid of some of them if I tried to visualize the emotions that accompanied them. I chose to respond to the belief that "If I am not exceptional and cannot fulfill expectations of others, I do not deserve to live."

Immediately a herd of giraffes came to mind and I asked them to explain to me why I had such a belief. They explained to me that it was necessary for me to be exceptional because my mother was under an enchantment and would turn into a horrible ugly creature if I did not work at being exceptional. When I demanded proof of their idea a baby giraffe befriended me and told me where to look for proof.

In my mind, I wandered through the woods until I came to a house where I saw my mother, my disturbed grandmother, and the woman who owned the house. My mother had brought my grandmother there to be in the country air and to recuperate from her mental illness. They were all playing cards. When my mother turned over the black jack (or the black joker), I knew it represented Teddy, her dead brother. At the sight of the card my mother grabbed it from the table and clasped it to her bosom with a cry of agony. Still in the visualization, I told the baby giraffe that I could see that it was my mother's attachment to Teddy that was the problem.

Coming out of the visualization, I was deeply upset. I realized at once that the fantasy was bringing to mind a real memory of the house to which my grandmother had been sent when she was suffering from a nervous breakdown following the death of her son, Teddy. Now in a state of semivisualization and real memory, I could "see" my grandmother in the house and could hear her screaming, "Why did you bring me here? Where am I? I want to go home!" It was terribly distressing to me to hear her and I wanted to force a pillow on her head to stop her from screaming. I remember that the woman's husband took me out into the garden to look at his flowers.

Suddenly I realized that I had a picture of this man and myself in a garden. So I understood that the visualization had allowed me to remember a frightening scene from the past, the memory of my grandmother during her mental breakdown. I vaguely remembered these visits and as a child I had often asked my mother about why Nana was sent away. She had always told me that she preferred not to talk about it.

This sequence of an emotionally charged fantasy about the giraffes and the card game, followed by the recall of a distressing childhood memory of my grandmother, provided the intuitive understanding about why I felt I had to be exceptional. My mother was "enchanted" by her morbid attachment to her dead brother, and I had to take his place. I had to be outstanding for all of them. I understood, too, why as a child I was afraid to challenge my mother's wishes. I had seen what had happened to my grandmother, and I did not want the same thing to happen to my mother. This was quite a burden for a young child to carry, and I had been carrying the burden for all of these years.

The point of recounting this rather complicated session with Sy is to show how my two therapies worked in complementary fashion. Didi started me with a focused visualization session about my mother, and she followed up with a discussion about the model of an ideal mother and an emphasis on how much my mother loved me. She spent as little time as possible on the past, and only to get some possible clues for action in the present. Sy followed me wherever I needed to go and was more patient than Didi with my excursions into my childhood. Sy also started with more assumptions about me than Didi did. He believed that I had to deal with my hostility to my mother in order to get rid of the guilt and the self-punitive attitudes. He had seen many examples of my categorical and negative thinking about myself and he wanted me to try to change this behavior. Didi, in contrast, was training me to find out what I wanted and then teaching me how to get it. She wanted me to develop my inner, untapped strengths and to reach out in an expansive way. Hers was an experiential more than a rational approach. But she also worked on changing my attitudes and my sense of the possible. Once we were beyond the serious work with my mother, the sessions with Didi often centered on the idea of how I was in the world in general, of my stern demands on myself and others. She, too, wanted me to expand out of the categorical but about different issues.

At the beginning of the second week Didi started me on my diary writing. Once shortly before, when I complained that there were so many things that were undone in my life, especially for my children, she gave me a large bound book containing manila drawing paper. She said that I could use it to draw or to write down my thoughts or keep a record of my therapy progress. It was to be a "gift" to my children of my experiences. In truth, the book was a special gift from Didi to me, because without the notes that I kept, I could never have written this story.

By the end of the first short phase of therapy that I have described in this chapter, Didi had started me on the road that reversed the process of the self-negating personality. She had begun with training in setting reasonable goals when she asked me to choose a date in the future that I wanted to live to. When I reached that goal in November it was one of the unforgettable moments of my life because it had been a reasonable goal and I had worked so hard to achieve it. The second step was to break the tie with my mother and to reverse the process of pleasing others. More than that, she turned my mother into a source of strength and support in my search for health. Although she assured me that the perfect mother did not exist, she supplied me with a relationship that had the qualities that I needed. She respected me as an individual and supported my healthy ways of being in the world. At the same time she retrained me to give up my destructive habits.

Neither Didi nor Sy suggested at this point that I try to learn to love myself. Stewart had emphasized this in his letters, and I certainly thought about what he had to say, but neither of them took this rather obvious path. Perhaps that is because, for both of them, retraining my sick personality was the real issue. They also assumed that if I succeeded in regaining psychological wholeness, the physical illness would be cured as well.

8

My Subpersonalities
Are Born

The second phase of therapy began with the creation of my subpersonalities. Didi began our work with several reading assignments. First I read a few chapters in Piero Ferrucci's book on psychosynthesis, *What We May Be*. These sections talked about the general ideas of the founder, Roberto Assagioli, about visualizations, wholeness, and will. Next she asked me to read the chapter on subpersonalities and finally gave me other readings for background on the subject. In the end I found Ferrucci's chapter, "A Multitude of Lives," to be the best.

The subpersonality represents different "models of the universe" that "color our perception and influence our way of being." For each we develop a different way of being in the world, different feelings, behaviors, words, habits, and beliefs. Each way represents an entire constellation of elements, like a miniature personality. The process for discovery is quite simple. Step one is to consider a prominent trait, attitude, or motive. Next, with eyes closed, one imagines an image to fit the trait. When the image is constant and a general feeling emanates from it, you let it talk, especially to tell you its needs. One then records the impression and the interaction and gives the subpersonality a name. You continue until as many subpersonalities are created as you need.

My first production was "Baby Alice." She started out as a representation of my incessant fearfulness. She is about two and a half years old, with straight brown hair and unattractive clothes. She knows that "Mother is always right." Her greatest desire in the world is to have a perfect mother and she will compromise her thoughts to have one. She wears short dresses and hates them; she also lies about her age. At first I always pictured her sitting in a corner crying.

Later, in discussions about her with Didi, I saw her on the porch of my house in Newark waiting for my father to come home on the bus. Here she was afraid because her mother was out playing bingo, and if her father arrived before her mother did, she would have to lie to him about her mother's whereabouts. When Didi heard this story she asked me what I (as grown-up Alice) would like to do to help her if I were a kind aunt in the family. I told her that I would handle the situation for her and tell my father the truth. Didi asked me to be especially nice to her and to try to make her less fearful by my promise to take care of her. It was through this figure and her need for a perfect mother that Didi and I discussed the concept of the perfect mother model and its impossibility of achievement.

Of the five major subpersonalities that I identified and used throughout therapy, Baby Alice underwent the most dramatic metamorphosis. But at the early stage of her development there was no indication of the malleability of her personality or any hint of the incredible strength she was to develop as therapy progressed.

I was caught up in the fun of creating subpersonalities so I moved on quickly to another one after the short work with Baby Alice. Next I chose a quality that was uppermost in my mind in the early days of therapy—the ability to manage hope. As a child I had learned to curb my imagination about future events because nothing ever worked out the way I had imagined it. Instead, I learned to depend on fate and the actions of others. I believed that this approach brought me the best of what life had to offer. But now everyone believed that it was important for me to have reasonable hope, and Sy was concerned that I not lapse into the feeling of hopelessness that had marked the period at the conclusion of the work on my Ph.D. Didi, without actually discussing the concept in general terms, had set me on the right path by the goal of extending my life until winter, but I still saw hope—or the lack thereof—as a quality that strongly defined my personality.

I sat quietly in my chair with my eyes closed and thought about the word *hope*. *No hope* and *hopelessness* came to mind in rapid succession. Suddenly I envisioned a crab running aimlessly on the beach, holding its front legs up in the air in a helpless manner. It was the only one of my subpersonalities that was masculine, at least in its original form. His story was as sad as his appearance. He belonged to a little gray-haired lady who spoke sweetly to him and always called him "dear." His *need* was to be free, but she tells him that this is impossible because she needs him to cut the woolen threads on a beautiful tapestry she is making. When he tells her of his dream to be free, she makes fun of him. When he asks what he can hope for, she laughs and tells him he can hope to be the flying horse in the tapestry. Every day he hopes to be the flying horse, but every evening he realizes that his hope is foolish and he runs around with his arms in the air bemoaning his fate and continuing to cut the threads for her.

I was very moved emotionally by the creation of this subpersonality so I continued with him for the remainder of the exercise. He was the first one that I took "up the mountain." According to Ferrucci, subpersonalities represent not only manifestations of traits, attitudes, or motives but may also be thought of as "degraded expressions of the archetypes of higher qualities." That is, humor descends to sarcasm, compassion becomes self-pity, or joy becomes mania. It is therefore not enough to identify and understand these aspects of self. Why not try to reverse the process and elevate these qualities? The theoretical bonus is that "the higher we rise, the closer we will be to unity. Conflict is among distortions—but there is no clash at the source." The facilitation of this process is aided by a deliberate image of ascent, i.e., of climbing a mountain. So I took the crab up the mountain.

We began, as per instruction, in a neutral place, in a meadow; we paused there to get a feel for the place. I always had my subpersonalities engage in certain activities in the meadow so that I could get a good idea of how they might change during the experience of ascent. In my meadow there were lots of flowers. It was an open field with trees on the northern boundary. If I faced south, I could see a small mountain. The sun was behind it and so its face was in the shade. The mountain was modest in size, like Barre Mountain, not far from my home. Up the shaded slope is a narrow and rocky trail that begins in easy steps but becomes very steep and difficult as it makes its way through the rocky ledges. About three quarters of the way up, on the east side of the mountain, there is a ledge that opens out to a view of a river and its valley far below. The final ascent is very difficult and gives one the impression of scaling a cliff. But at the top of the mountain there is a small flat area where the sun is shining.

The crab had little trouble climbing up the mountain, scurrying on ahead of me in a rather frantic way. When I saw that he was going out on the ledge, I became very frightened for him, knowing his desperation and his deep desire to be free. And sure enough, before I could reach him he jumped off in a gleeful manner. When I reached the ledge I expected to see his mutilated body below. But instead I saw a Baltimore oriole flying about and singing beautifully. He never did realize his dream of becoming a flying horse, but as a bird he perched on my shoulder and sang so sweetly that I knew he was happy.

Oriole stayed with the other subpersonalities throughout our other journeys up the mountain and was with us when we all finally learned to fly. I don't recall any dramatic change accompanying this experience, but in retrospect I think I understand what was happening. Oriole, in his crab form, represented my relationship with my mother, who would never really let me fly and for whom I had a deep sense of responsibility. In other words, I knew that I played a very important part in supporting her own unrealistic fantasies. At the same time I knew that I could never satisfy her completely because I was not her little brother who had died at a young age. She often laughed at me, made fun of my maturing female body, and teased and goaded me into action by calling me "Mousey." She would take me to school by car and wait with me until the last bell rang. As I walked away she would call after me, "Good-bye, Mousey." Even when I asked her not to do it she would laugh and call all the louder. Hence, my relationship with her was a true trap from which I could see no escape; hence, the sense of hopelessness, which was carried over to all my relationships and to my way of being in the world.

Perhaps this exercise freed me in a way that I was not aware of. Perhaps, as well as giving up the goal of a perfect mother, I also gave up the foolish fantasy that things would be better with my mother if I were a boy. The transformation of the helpless crab to the little bird seems quite appropriate also if one recalls Emily Dickinson's description of hope just this way—of a little bird on one's shoulder. So this transformation represents a more mature attitude about hope: I changed it from a sad impossible dream to something within the realm of possibility.

Moving on to other aspects of myself, I identified "Amanda, the builder." She arose out of my love of designing houses and rooms. I designed our home and addition, and sometimes when I am distressed I amuse and distract myself by reading about new house designs. I viewed her as a strong woman with thick, coarse blond hair. Her needs are simple: she requires only the tools of her trade and the lumber to construct the houses. She makes beautiful little cottages in the woods, with stone fireplaces and wooden furniture. When she is finished she leaves the house for some unknown persons to occupy. She is strong and independent and does not need the feedback or admiration of other people. Her greatest satisfaction is solely in the process of construction.

Amanda's image was essential to me in changing attitudes that I knew were destructive but which I found hard to shake. For instance, during the crucial six weeks I am describing, Sy and I had to make a trip to our condominium at Killington, Vermont, to make minor repairs and to replace any dishes or other equipment that might have been lost or taken during the winter rental months. Killington had sometimes been a bone of contention between Sy and me, as I often viewed it as a burden more than a pleasure. As our daughters grew up and went on with their own lives, we spent less and less time there as a family. I hated the constant time spent cleaning or fixing it up, and I especially hated cleaning up the mess that other people had made.

Didi and I had discussed my negative attitude about the place and more about my constant habit of not enjoying each experience for what it was worth. She told me that she, too, had to learn to enjoy the moment and to say to herself constantly, "This is enough." So I went to Killington that weekend repeating over and over again, "This is enough." The result of this concerted effort to change my attitude was that I had a very enjoyable time.

I used this stratagem for other attitudes too. I thought of Amanda as someone who could do anything. I chanted to myself constantly when I tended to be negative or complaining, "I am Amanda, and I am strong. I am Amanda, and I am strong—and this is enough, this moment with Sy is enough!" And it worked! Not only for this but for any time when I felt sorry for myself. I also used this image as I walked through the woods and thought of "killing the cancer cells" in my body. "I am Amanda. I am strong! Kill the cancer! Kill the cancer, kill the cancer! *I am Amanda. I am strong.*"

Although the three subpersonalities that I have just described are somewhat interesting and a little pathetic with their sad stories, they lack emotional flavor and intensity. Not so with the last two in my subpersonality gallery, "Little One" and "Mickey." There is little indication in my notes what trait I had in mind when I conjured up Little One, but I assume that I was thinking about my sharp temper and the hostility and rage that I often felt but rarely expressed. Every once in a while, though, the temper would come out. As a young woman I expressed my anger by shouting at Sy when he did things that frustrated me, such as coming home late when we were entertaining. Sometimes I yelled at the kids, but not too often. As I got older I let out my frustration by going to the "screaming hill" just a little way from the house. Sometimes the children or my niece, Donna, would join me and we would all have a good yell.

Assuming that I was trying to express this volatile part of

myself, Little One came to mind. She is a tiny, lithe little dancer who frequently wears a witch mask with a large ugly nose. She walks hunched over—not in submission but in an expression of the wonderful schemes she is hatching to get back at people. She is nasty, aggressive, devious, and joyously happy about her evil thoughts and deeds. She throws back her head and laughs a lot. She pushes, kicks, stabs, claws, spits, bites, strangles, beats with a club, punches, etc., and then runs away. She never gets caught. She hates Baby Alice and thinks she is stupid and worthy only of contempt. I hate to admit that I liked her from the beginning, but I did.

Such an interesting character elicited my interest so I developed her further by taking her up the mountain. In the meadow she was very destructive, stamping on the wildflowers (lady's slipper, columbine, adder's-tongue, all delicate gems) and pushing around Baby Alice and taunting her. She was killing chipmunks and rabbits by strangling them, smashing them, throwing dirt at them, and then laughing.

On the way up Little One scrambles over the boulders with amazing agility, which amazes Baby Alice and me. She (Little One) goes on ahead, appearing at unexpected places, scaring and surprising us, and also pushing boulders down on us, hoping to hurt us. When her mask becomes too hot with all this activity, she throws it off. We can now see her beautiful black curly hair and her bright blue eyes. She sticks her tongue out at us, but up ahead quite a distance, she tires and lies down on a cool place near the ledge to rest. I know that she is looking down at the view of the valley where the hawks are flying. She sleeps soundly, and when she awakens she has been transformed into a beautiful tiger named Bagera. She is strong, powerful, but not unduly aggressive. She is proud of her sleek coat and her beauty. She is now more straightforward in her aggression, which is more justified. In other words, she may kill, but only to eat. The most surprising thing is that when we all reach the top, she lets Baby Alice ride on her back, at least for a while. She likes herself much better now.

I guess that Little One is pretty transparent: she is all of my unbridled hostility turned outward. Most important, however, is the intuitive sense that I knew that I didn't have anything to fear from her. I admired her and now had some real insight of how she could be tamed. Her antagonism to Baby Alice is extreme, but I guess all of the conforming attitudes went into Baby Alice while Little One had the absolute opposite. They were thus destined to be enemies as long as they both remained undeveloped. But the trip up the mountain told me—although I didn't realize it at the time—that they could be reunited through making them more developed and mature. That process was a long way off. The important thing was that I had a succinct manifestation of two of my most important characteristics, knowing what each wanted and how to begin to satisfy them.

Perhaps this work on the subpersonalities above was in preparation for the most complicated and problematic one of all, Mickey. Mickey was the manifestation of jealousy: she is a jealous little girl with red curly hair who longs to be Shirley Temple. No one likes her because she is critical of what everyone else does. She wants to be admired and liked by her own playmates. But they do not like her because she wants their things and eventually gets them by tricking them. She wants attention from the boys but they do not like her either. When they mention other girls that they do like, she finds fault with them. The boys end up picking on her and throwing things at her.

In the valley she looks at all the beautiful wildflowers and keeps saying that what she has at home is more beautiful. I see the wildflowers swaying in the breeze when she is in the valley. On the way up the mountain she runs ahead at first but gets tired very quickly, and another group of children starting out behind her and proceeding slowly easily pass her by. She follows them, but the path becomes very hard. She climbs to the same ledge that Little One was on when she turned into a tiger. She, however, turns into a chicken, and like Chicken Little of storybook fame, she goes around telling everyone that the sky will fall.

At this point I stopped the exercise of creating subpersonalities and rested from what had been almost an hour of work, reading, visualizing, and writing. I may have even meditated a little, as was my practice in the afternoon. Then I began to think about the creatures of my visualizations. Mickey especially intrigued me, as I read over what I had written about her, and I decided to work on her some more. First of all, her name: Why was she called Mickey? That was the name my father called me as a young child. I remember that I used to like it very much when he called me Mickey because it meant that I was someone special to him. I have no doubt that on some level this was true: I was his only child for six years and he spent time with me, putting me to bed at night, reading me the Sunday funnies, and taking me to the park. I suspect that the name represented my diminutive stature as well as an affectionate appellation. On the other hand, he might well have taken it from the cartoon creature Mickey Mouse, who was popular when I was growing up. In this context perhaps it was not so complimentary. Perhaps in some sense it also showed that on a less conscious level, he viewed me as someone too eager, too cute?

Although I was unable to solve this riddle, I was intrigued by it, and so I continued my thoughts about Mickey. I reasoned that in some sense she was the part of

me that was hidden, at least to all but the most astute observers. Most people who know me casually would probably
describe me as warm, cooperative, helpful, and generous to
a fault. Only perhaps later would they begin to sense the
competitiveness and hear the subtle criticism come out.
Some people might never get behind my carefully created
facade but might be left with a sense of discomfort that they
could never understand. Mickey, then, was the part of me
that I was most eager to keep hidden from other people
because her characteristics were so opposite to the me that I
wanted to project and that I wanted to believe I was. But in
my heart I must admit I feared that the "good" me was just
a cover for the "real" me that was like Mickey.

More than the frightened Baby Alice or the passionate
Little One, Mickey was the skeleton in my closet. She represented many secret fears. She reminded me of the fear that I
would never amount to anything in the world, that although
I always started out ahead of my competitors, in the long
run I would always lose out. She was the part of me that
feared that she would never be satisfied, the part with the
unattainable dream. She was the me who, before I became
ill, feared that Sy could never really love me unless I played
the role of the good and accommodating wife. Moreover,
since she lived in fear of exposure, she avoided direct confrontation most of all and had to accomplish her goals in a
sneaky way. It then became clear why she changed into
Chicken Little: She was literally afraid that "the sky would
fall" if she were found out.

With all of this in mind, I decided to try to take her up
the mountain once more. I saw her first in the field of wildflowers again, but before I could take her up the path, she
changed into a giant chicken that I was afraid might acci-
dentally hurt me just because of her size. Then suddenly, as
if expressing my secret fear, she came running after me as if

she were purposely trying to kill me. The more I ran, the faster she came, with a confident strutting motion that I had seen in some real chickens in a barnyard once. I became desperate as I realized that I had to stop her, but I didn't know how!

In my growing panic there was a terrible new insight: "This is the part of me that wants me dead! How will I stop her?" I somehow sensed that there was some word that she wanted to hear and that the word was *forgive*. So I turned to her and screamed, "I forgive you!" To my horror, she did not stop, but instead turned into a huge vampire bat and came straight for me. I had no choice; I wrestled her down and stabbed her to death. I came out of the visualization shaken but satisfied.

The next day in therapy, when I told Didi about this encounter, she became very disturbed—practically the only time that she ever reacted this way to me. She shook her head and said sternly, "I don't ever want you to kill anything again. It shouldn't be necessary." I was not daunted, however, because at last I knew where the self-destruction was located and I felt that defeating it in the Mickey form was good for me. I told her defiantly that I would try to heed her warning but that I was glad I had done it. Her response was that we should talk about Mickey some more if I felt up to it.

Didi asked me to become as calm as possible and to visualize Mickey, if I could, as a young girl. I saw her as a young girl of about six years old fixing up her room. She is wearing a red flowered dress. She is crying because the new baby's crib is going to be put into her room and she hates the idea of losing her own room. She tells the adults that she thinks it will be nice to have her new sister there, but it is not true. She tries to be helpful to everyone. She goes around telling everyone how much the baby cries, how she doesn't like the way it smells—but all in a joking manner.

After this brief visualization we talked about Mickey in a rational way. I described her as always tense, stuttering a lot, and with a sinking feeling in her stomach. She has a slightly stuck-up expression on her face, which shows her disdain for the world. She dresses in a special way, wearing very short dresses that her mother picks out for her. It is an attention-getting device that has both good and bad aspects. She liked to show other people how great she is; she is a show-off when she thinks she can do well. She wants recognition for her superiority. When she is in control of my life, I am very tense. Mickey is very insecure and thinks that having special privileges is a way to find the security she wants. She is self-centered and makes reality fit her needs.

She wants a great many things but is afraid to ask for them because she fears refusal more than anything. She is afraid that someone will say no. She is afraid to be embarrassed; she is afraid to appear grasping; she doesn't know when or how to just make her needs known. She becomes furious when someone tells her that she doesn't have a right to do something or be somewhere. Yet, often when she gets what she works and wheedles for, she finds that she doesn't want it anymore. She built a house at Eastman to find a community that she thought she could not find in Amherst, but when she got there she didn't like it at all.

The Mickey part of me emerges in all comparison situations, at school, at social gatherings, with Sy, with my children, and especially with Ruth. She began to emerge when I was a child, and has been a dominant part of my personality for the past twenty years. She was at her worst in Switzerland and during my work on my Ph.D.

Mickey's relationship to my other subpersonalities is generally hostile. She and the builder, Amanda, are antagonists;

she and Little One hate each other and actually fight; but she does get along just fine with Baby Alice. It is good that she has at least one friend, although I don't see why it is Baby Alice.

Didi was very sympathetic to the Mickey personality and asked me to try to find redeeming qualities in her. I responded with a list of more shortcomings as I emphasized the destructive aspect of her fantastic energy. She is completely motivated by other people, either to do things that they indicate they would like to have done or by things they suggest I do to make them happy. Her neurotic needs to make things nice urged me on to build a stone wall in our first house even though the stones were too heavy and, if I had waited a few weeks, Sy would have helped me. Her energy built the house in Eastman at a time when Sy was having back problems and didn't want to be bothered at first. She also started me on my Ph.D. fiasco because she thought that Sy wanted me to do it and she kept me at the task long after any sensible person would have quit. I disparaged both her tendency to want to quit and her tenacity in sticking to a path that was self-destructive. I saw few strengths in her and I hated her for bringing me to this point in my life.

Didi refused to give up. "Alice," she said, "try to keep in mind that this personality is a child who has been hurt and is responding in the only way she knows how. It is your job to love her and to satisfy her needs in a straightforward manner so that she doesn't have to be devious or always feel jealous. Don't you see that?" I conceded that I understood where she wanted me to go, but I was not ready to take the next step. "How can I love someone who is trying to kill me?" I asked. "Right now, I hate her!"

We ended on this note and went on to discuss other things. As I left Didi's house I felt that I had accomplished a great deal of work during the session and during the past few days. I was correct. We had now switched into a new gear in psychotherapy. We were beginning to talk about self-love. Not as an amorphous quality, but as a specific reaction to a not-so-lovable part of my personality. The power of this approach was that I had identified other aspects of myself that I could love and respect, so the job was limited.

We had also taken the first steps in rebuilding my psyche; that is, we had identified its components, strengths, and weaknesses. There wasn't too much yet to build on, but I imagine that Amanda could be considered part of the small personality core that sustained me. Notice, however, that she represented sheer force of will, and inner strength, but had no ability to interact with people on the outside world. Little One, too, can be viewed as a source of some strength because a part of me could still feel a sense of wrong and wanted revenge. She was useless to express this wrong except in immature outbursts, but at least she was likable.

I do not know what the usual sequence of events would have been following the identification of these personality parts, but I put them to good use immediately in helping me to make an important decision.

9

A Crucial Decision

At this point in my life there were several issues in the real world that I had to resolve. One was the problem of deciding which interferon program to go to, the one at Boston or the one that Marty and Toby had told me about in New Haven. The second was the growing tension between Sy and me over whether I should start any physical therapy at all.

Despite the fact that I had been put off by the thought of going to Boston for the gamma interferon program, when Marty and Toby told me about the alternative alpha program in New Haven, I was interested. The programs differed in several ways besides their location and a slightly different form of interferon. The Boston program was using a more recent type of interferon that seemed to be somewhat more powerful (about 40 percent effective), but they were in an earlier stage of the experiment in which the main goal was to test dosage level. Hence they were using strong doses that required hospitalization for two weeks and had produced some strong side effects, mostly severe flu-like symptoms and some reversible kidney and liver dysfunction. However, there was an excitement about the researchers in Boston that was attractive. All the patients were in a special part of the hospital under the direct surveillance of the research staff. I liked the fact that I would be putting myself into the hands of the staff as I had during my recent surgery.

In contrast the New Haven program had only a 25 percent response rate but did not require hospitalization. As a matter of fact, there they taught you to self-administer the drug. That was scary to me since I'm very queasy about needles. However, I assumed that if I couldn't bring myself to inject the drug, either Sy would do it for me or I could go to my local HMO to have it administered by a nurse when I needed it. New Haven was attractive further because it was about thirty minutes from where Marty and Toby lived in Cheshire, Connecticut. Marty accompanied me on my first visit to the clinic and proposed that I could use her home as a way station before or after the therapy. Besides, although the staff was wonderful at both places, I felt more comfortable with Dr. Ernstoff in New Haven because he was very open in discussing all the other programs for renal-cell cancer.

There was another issue that was important to me—the cost and how it would be covered. The Boston program was very expensive, and because of the experimental aspect of both programs, coverage by some health programs was dubious. I became all mixed up about how much of the family resources I could expect to use up on my treatment, in case the HMO would not cover my expenses. Decisions were made case by case, and there had even been a question of whether the HMO would cover my trip to New Haven for diagnosis. They had already completely covered my diagnostic trip to Boston and all of my surgery bills.

In some sense this was a wonderful prototypical problem for all of my subpersonalities to solve. There was the issue of dependence versus independence in the administration of the drug; there was the issue of what the statistical percent cures meant and how much weight to put on that; there was the issue of how much I thought my cure might be worth in monetary terms; and the final issue was to see what was best for me—not Sy, not the children, but just for me.

But this was not all, because I began to detect a subtle pressure from Sy (at least I interpreted it to be so) not to go for any physical therapy at all. It was strange to me since he had been so positive about the Boston experience at first. Yet, as the time for a decision came, I began to sense that he wanted me to try the psychological approach longer. It had been about a month since my last X ray, when they had discovered that there was a second lesion in my lungs and when the oncologist told me that I had three months to live. Sy, therefore, urged me to have another X ray to see if there had been any change in my condition one way or the other. I refused. The Hindu guru had said not to look too often, once the healing process had been begun, and I wanted to follow this. Also I was afraid to have another X ray, to see the awful reality of those cold pictures. I was feeling better physically every day, and in some sense I was afraid that it would set me back to see them if they were worse. Despite Didi's training to look at the medical results as only one aspect of reality, it was a powerful negative stimulus to overcome.

I began to be very disturbed about Sy's attitude, which I saw in financial terms alone. I believed that he didn't want me to go to the interferon treatment because of its possible financial burden, when in reality I think he was most concerned about the possible side effects causing me real damage. He was also impatient with my refusal to take a scientific approach and find out what, if anything, was really happening. Things became tense between us for one of the first times since my illness, and I began to think that he was withdrawing his affection from me at a time when I needed it the most. Sy and I began to resolve this ourselves with one of our famous evening discussions.

I started with a tirade against Sy for withdrawing his affection from me because we disagreed about the treatment. I dragged up old stuff about his lack of affection for me when we disagreed on some basic issue. I told him how wonderful it must be when two people really are in synchrony with each other. I told him how much I admire older couples who enjoy doing simple things together. With us it is different—we always do what he wants to do or we do nothing. I went on and on, getting more emotional and more angry. All that I needed now was for Sy to say some little wrong thing and I would be off in a huff, closing the discussion and accusing him of controlling me by assuming the role of a therapist. Perhaps that did happen, I don't remember, but at some stage in the discussion Sy looked very puzzled and said, "Wait a minute, Alice. Do you really believe that I love you less when we disagree?" I said, "Of course real love means that you agree on goals even if you may not always agree on methods, and here we have different goals and I have a very difficult time opposing you. I want us to have the same goal so that my decision will be easier."

He shook his head and said, "Well, I think that you have it all wrong. We can disagree on goals and still love each other very much, in fact even more. I'll also tell you that I do not intend to be bullied by you into changing my opinion to make your decision easier. What I will promise you is that, despite what you think, I will support you when you finally make up your mind whether I would do it that way or not. If you don't believe that after all these years, then I don't know what I can say to make you believe it."

I realized that I had hurt him with my accusations but somehow that didn't matter too much to me. Somehow

what came over me was that I had one view of what consti-
tuted love and he had a completely different one. It was
strange because I had always assumed that there could be
no other view than the one I had. Somehow, at this moment, I realized that I could respect this difference, not
deciding who was right or wrong. And, for the first time, I
could believe that his future support was not contingent
upon our agreeing. I knew in my heart that he had made a
commitment to me to back me no matter what I decided
and so all I had to do was to make up my mind, to find out
just what I wanted. For once I had been honest, without the
buffer of my temper or deviousness or tears to make my
point. It was a very emotional moment. We both knew that
something new had entered our lives. I put my arms around
him and we held each other. In the past I would have told
him how much I loved him so that he wouldn't be angry
with me and our difference would be hidden once more. But
I knew that it was not necessary anymore. My work was cut
out for me with Didi. I had to examine this ideal model of
love that I had carried around for all these years, and I had
to decide for myself which interferon treatment to take, if
any.

The ongoing experience with Didi began to change the
way I viewed many things. She continually questioned all
my assumptions about how the world was supposed to be
and kept pointing out that what I believed was undesirable
could have other interpretations. My tendency to always
talk in terms of the final outcome changed slowly to an
interest in the process of the journey. My tendency to be
pessimistic and critical changed to a broader appraisal of
possibilities and the establishment of both a more benign
outlook and one that used my own criteria, not society's or
that of some authority figure.

As a consequence of broadening my view of each situation, my past errors became obvious to me. I realize now that I had started out correctly in our marriage, trying to satisfy my needs as well as Sy's. But I gave up too easily when things did not come out the way I thought they should. I was too insecure to hold out, to bargain. So, before I knew it, Sy became a substitute for my mother—his needs became mine. I was also burdened with some unreasonable needs such as my search for the ideal mother and the ideal husband—perhaps rolled into one. I assumed that the model of behavior that I had experienced with my mother was universal, that I would be rejected if I viewed the world differently from her, so I never gave Sy a chance to show that he could be different. Instead, when my first attempts at compromise or demand didn't work out, I said, "Okay, I must see things through his eyes and do only what he wants to do."

The incident with Sy began a reverse snowballing effect that led me to healthy behavior. In the past I had kept narrowing my possibilities and his possible reactions until neither of us had room to move. It resulted not only in my unhappiness but, as he has now admitted, in an uneasiness in him that he never could satisfy me and that in any situation—a party, a vacation—I could become dissatisfied for reasons he couldn't understand. Yes, I knew that in a really critical situation, Sy always came through for me when I needed him, but I believed that I couldn't use that card too much or it would lose its power.

Now I see Sy as a normal, casual person who will look out for his own interest and take the easy way out if he can. He will ask for help if he needs it, and if I am stupid enough to sacrifice my own welfare for his, he will accept my sacrifice. He is very involved in his own work, at which he is very successful and which gives him great joy and stimulation. He is too involved in himself most of the time to worry about whether I am satisfied. But I notice that he is very pleased when I do find fulfillment in my own tasks.

Although I certainly did not have the understanding of myself that I have now, as the weeks of therapy rolled on I was gaining confidence in my ability to operate in the world with more personal power and with results that made me happier. In other words, I had some practice in good decision-making before I had to make the all-important decision about my treatment. I also had the conceptualization of my subpersonalities to fall back on. In the middle of the effort to decide which therapy to try, I decided that I would turn to my subpersonalities for help. Reading over what I had written about each one, I wrote down what each would decide. Baby Alice definitely voted for Boston because she would be taken care of there and I had promised to get the best for her. In terms of facilities and the higher response rate, Boston was the "best." Oriole opted for New Haven and I can't remember why. Amanda obviously would pick New Haven because this program trained me in independence. Mickey, like Baby Alice, wanted to go to Boston, and Little One told me that these things were out of her range of interest or expertise and that I shouldn't bother her about it anymore.

So with a tied vote among my subpersonalities, I walked into therapy knowing that the decision had to be made immediately. Didi said very little as I reviewed the arguments pro and con, including the emotional reasons for each side. But as I went on with my arguments I realized that she was exhibiting an intense concentration that I had never seen before, listening with all of her faculties, both rational and emotional. I had just finished talking about Boston in the most positive way when I suddenly heard myself saying, "On the other hand, if I could get myself to go to New Haven, it would be the best growth experience that I will ever have. Imagine, if I could really learn to give myself the injections, it would mean that we could still travel if we wanted to and I would be so much more independent."

Didi spoke for the first time in about five minutes as she told me, "Well, it is interesting to me, Alice, that I was just about to tell you that what I was hearing was that you really wanted to go to Boston, and then I heard a switch, and right now it sounds as if New Haven is the place you really want. Think about it some more and we'll talk more if you need to."

That night I went back to my subpersonalities once more to review their arguments, and interestingly Little One had made up her mind too. She said that it was really simple now for her, looking over all of the other responses. Since Baby Alice and Mickey wanted to go to Boston, and she had so little respect for either one of them, she could now vote for New Haven with a clear conscience. That was it as far as I was concerned, and the next morning I called Boston and said that I would not be coming. Following this, I made my arrangements with the Yale–New Haven Hospital to come within a week.

It was not that easy, however, to begin the experimental therapy because I had to go through a series of tests to tell them what my situation was like before treatment, repetitions of those I had taken before my operation. They needed a bone scan to see if the bone tissue was involved, another CAT scan to see if the primary area had further complications, a chest X ray to finally look at my lungs, and blood work.

Since my HMO wanted to do as much of the testing as possible in their own facilities, we tried to make arrangements at the local hospital. The bone scan was no problem and an appointment was arranged immediately. The radiologist knew me from a preoperative procedure that my surgeon, Dr. Miller, had ordered, and much to my surprise, as I waited for final clearance after the test, he came out to tell me that the bone scan was still negative, as it had been in the original battery of diagnostic tests. I was most appreciative for this information and for his concern, which went beyond the usual medical protocol. The CAT scan, however, was different; appointments were impossible to get with the mobile unit in our area and even Yale–New Haven couldn't take me in time. There was a private clinic in New Haven that did find an appointment for me, but even this meant a postponement of the therapy for an extra week. Finally I was scheduled to begin just after Memorial Day, on June 2.

On the week before that date Lisa and I drove to New Haven for the CAT scan and the blood work. I hand-carried the result of the CAT scan to the oncology department at Yale–New Haven Hospital. In my new boldness, I insisted that the nurse read it and tell me the results. She opened the package and read and reread the message over several times. She finally said, "I don't understand this. They say that the area is cancer free." I explained to her that the lungs were the main area of concern now, not the original site, but I could hardly contain my excitement to find out that the original site was clear. My original oncologist had said that the primary site was probably deteriorating as well. But now, after almost three months, it was fine.

I returned home in good spirits because of this information and because of my very positive experience at the clinic. While getting the blood work done, I saw other patients having their treatments and I liked the general atmosphere in the place. I felt a sharp contrast now to the sense of futility that I had experienced just six weeks before in the oncologist's office. I knew that I was ready psychologically and physically for the treatments to begin, having resolved my doubts and having Sy's complete backing for the project. But beyond these changes, I was dramatically aware that I had grown in spirit to a level that I would never have imagined possible.

10

Spiritual Leaps

My spiritual growth was nurtured by my meditations, subtle encouragement from Didi, and my contacts with Lisa, Anna, and Stewart. It developed at the same time that I changed psychologically. Both processes, I believe, were essential to my eventual recovery.

When I talk about spirituality I am referring to feelings that transcend the self and the ordinary material world. A deep religious feeling would certainly be in this category, or an intense reaction to the beauty of nature: seeing a rainbow, watching the ocean, or being thrilled by the birth of a child. Often these moments are followed by an intense feeling of love. I believe that they are produced by a unique moment of integration and a temporary loss of self. I think that in an extended form, they may be the essence of healing.

At first there was no organization to what I was doing on the spiritual level. I knew, however, that the readings and special meditations of myself in light made me feel good so I continued. Then, after three or four weeks, as I became accustomed to what had been strange and foreign ideas, patterns began to emerge.

ADVICE FROM STEWART ON HEALING

Stewart called me every week and sent me letters, which more and more contained direct mention of his beliefs about God and in-depth ideas about how to enhance my healing. He always ended with the strong admonition to love myself, to keep in mind a healthy body (shining, glowing, vibrant with life and light). Soon he began to speak of the importance of being able to manifest God's grace in order to change the structure of things. This was not a matter of force of will, he pointed out, but the ability to unfold and to ask for grace. He encouraged me to talk to God as I would to a close friend. He told me that because of our God-given free will, it is impossible for God to come to us uninvited.

In later letters Stew wrote about "claiming an inner opulence that is your birthright as a child of God." He asked me to try to make contact with my inner being, which, according to him, is not subject to pain or to death. "This part of you existed before you were born and will exist after you die. The Eastern people call it the astral body. Remember, the power to heal does not come from yourself, but from an enlarging of the boundaries of self that includes others and the mystery and miracle of love that is greater than all of us. Love is always there, but your new receptiveness will let it in."

THE ELEMENTS OF SELF-HEALING

After a while the readings from Yogananda and from David Spangler's *The Laws of Manifestation* began to form a somewhat unified message. There were three spiritual elements of self-healing that were mentioned over and over: openness, self-love, and faith. I began to assess my progress toward these goals. I knew I had developed openness: I listened to what everyone said and used my growing confidence in my intuition to decide what was right for me. I was working on loving myself: I was struggling to love all of my subpersonalities and I saw my body in light every time I meditated. Faith, however, was much harder to come by. David Spangler said, "You must not lose faith in the fact that you will be healed, because it is faith that is the vehicle by which you change the reality that you created over the past." I tried, but my natural pessimism made faith very problematic for me.

SPANGLER'S SPECIAL MESSAGE

The more I read, the more I understood, so I began to concentrate on the very difficult passages in David Spangler's book *The Laws of Manifestation.* He is very specific about the stages of making one's desires manifest. After one develops openness, a sense of attunement to God, and a sense of intuitive knowing, it is time to examine one's needs and to try to give them form. Most important here is that the need not be thought of as requesting a specific favor but as the symbol of what God is trying to express through you. Once you have an image of what you are striving for, you then support this image with positive thought (faith), which makes it real. The last stage in the manifestation is to give thanks, which in essence is acknowledging the whole from which the manifestation comes.

Although I was beginning to comprehend what Spangler was saying, I experienced new frustration because I could think of no elevated way to express my desire to be well, and of course I still had no faith. I continued to meditate and to read, still lacking the essential ingredient for manifesting health, until a series of events happened that made me understand.

ANNA'S LETTER

About the middle of May, Anna and her mother, Gerry, came for a visit that left me feeling strong emotionally and physically. After returning to New York, Anna wrote me a wonderful letter. She told me that my struggles in therapy and against the illness reminded her of struggles with her own psychological ghosts. She wrote that I should try not to be discouraged by some periods of failure and fear. "Fear really is the opposite of faith," she wrote, "and faith is not something we find and then keep, but a choice that needs to be made at each moment. Choose to keep your mind on all the powerful, wonderful, universal energy that you have within you. For lack of a better word, I call that God. You are a creation of this loving energy that is both within you and all around you—you can claim its help as your own by *simply asking for it.*"

While Anna's letter contained some important new ideas, its real importance for me was that it reinforced many key concepts that I was hearing from other sources, such as the need for faith, the need to ask for help, and the idea of contacting a force that is your heritage, your connection with the universal. This brought to mind what Stewart had written about the astral body, my connection to the life force.

A SPECIAL MEDITATION

One day, after a particularly deep meditation, it occurred to me that the concept of the astral self was the image that I needed to make manifest my healing. I decided to try to make contact with the universal part of myself, the source of life and love. I chose a time when no one would bother me and started to meditate. I saw myself in light as I always did, but kept the image longer than usual. Then I began to think of this astral self, the eternal part of me. In my mental image I was standing on the top of a sunlit hill with my arms outstretched, reaching to the sky. I begged for help. I asked over and over for this force to help me to live, for it to receive me, to touch me, to give me the strength I needed. I didn't pray or bargain. I just asked for contact. I did it with the most intense longing that I could muster. I didn't release myself into it; I sought it with the greatest force of will that I could produce.

I must have meditated deeply for over an hour. As with such meditation, one begins to get a feeling of separation from body. First I lost the sense of touch in my hands. I knew that they were touching a pillow but this sensation was no longer there. Then I began to lose the sense of the contact with the chair, and a lightness occurred that was pleasant. Sounds then ceased to exist, the background sounds disappeared, and I began to have a sense of existing out of time and space.

By now the pleading, the intensity, had stopped, and I was left with a wonderful sense of well-being. In this state I suddenly felt something light and soft brush across my right cheek. It lasted for quite a while so that it was hard to ignore, but I managed to absorb it into my state and within fifteen minutes I ended the meditation. All in all, I was pleased with the meditation, although this is not usually an evaluation that I make. It was a special experience.

But what of the strange feeling on my face? My logical mind forced me to seek some physical explanation for the sensation that I had felt. I looked for some little piece of lint on my face or an insect, a small spider that might have lowered itself on a filament from the beam above. There was nothing, nowhere. Suddenly I was overcome with an emotion that was hard to contain. Tears came into my eyes, and I began to say to myself, "Oh, you didn't ask for a sign, not this time, you purposely didn't ask for a sign, but you got one."

The feeling passed, and I went about my business in the house. After supper I meditated again, and then reread the passage about faith and knowing, the all-important step in the process of manifestation. I knew that I had an image of the astral self to ask for help. What now of the "faith born of knowledge" that the manifestation would happen. Faith born of knowledge—that strange combination came to my mind again. And then it all made sense. Of course, my experience of the afternoon was it. I did know. I did have knowledge that I hadn't had before. I didn't know when, or how, or how long, or whether I would be sicker before I got better, but I believed that I would be well. I finally understood about faith and I understood deep inside me that I had it.

A NEW VISUALIZATION

I never tried to reproduce the meditation of that special day. But I was boosted by this experience, by my progress in therapy with my subpersonalities, and by my ability to move directly and effectively in the world. I therefore had a new feeling as I moved into the last few days of waiting before the interferon therapy was to begin.

My meditations continued on a strict schedule and followed a specific routine. Ever since early in therapy and the visualization with the elephant, I had changed my anticancer visualization from white knights in a jousting arena to a spaceship operating with a powerful beam of light. This was part of the realization that I had to take a new perspective, to approach my problems from a new level.

I now viewed my body from above in the spaceship. With great difficulty at first, I forced the ship into three dimensions, above, below—and most complicated—around, getting at every surface of the lung lesions with the beam. I watched the edges of the mass disintegrate into tiny pieces, a little at a time. Every day I could see that the mass was smaller and the intense work at the surface was paying off. I went inside my body with the beam as well, to get rid of any cancer cells in my blood and at the site of the original growth in my abdomen.

Every day I continued like this, until it was the Sunday before I was to go. Without actually talking about the fact that it should be a special day, we decided to spend the afternoon on the Connecticut River; Sy fished and I just enjoyed the peace and calm of being on the water. As we got out of the boat to return home, Sy pulled me to him and held me. It was as if in this moment we were drawn to each other by some unspoken need to hold on to this moment and to each other. I did not ask him what he was thinking, but I knew what was on my mind. I knew that life would never be the same for us again. There was no way of knowing what my reaction would be to the interferon or what was ahead. But I was ready to face my future, and the faith was still there that I would somehow be well.

11

A Short Reprieve

Monday came, and it was time for me to go to New Haven and begin the interferon program. We arrived at the hospital about ten o'clock in the morning. On the way down we talked about what I could expect from the all-important chest X ray. Everything else had tested out negative, so the results on my chest were particularly important as an indication of my present condition. Sy had emphasized to me again that the results of the X ray really were moot, since the treatment was systemic. Two spots or ten would be just the same. This concept was further reinforced when we met another patient, a staff physician, who was also starting the interferon program. He had refused to even have his cancerous kidney removed because, he told us, he believed the treatment could be extremely effective in reducing the disease.

The first step was to fill out the ominous agreement to begin the experimental therapy. I was shocked and frightened to discover exactly what it meant to participate in such a program. Some of the side effects, such as infections or heart disturbances, were possibly life-threatening. There were also some reversible effects to other organs and the chance of hair loss, nausea, and mental confusion. I hastily signed the papers; I had come this far and I knew I had no other option.

Next we were sent to the main building for my chest X ray. I was tempted to open the large manila envelope on the spot and look at it, but it was sealed. By the time we returned several patients had arrived and the waiting room suddenly became very crowded. We waited for a while longer, and finally they showed us to a viewing room, where the technician placed the present X ray on the screen. I didn't want to look, but I did.

I was disoriented as I looked at the screen, but I could see a large circular spot on my right lung and about twenty-five more down the center of the screen. "Oh no," I cried to myself, "it has spread! Both lungs are now infected along two lines down the middle of my body." My heart began to beat faster, and then something inside me took over. I told myself not to lose heart. I was truly in an altered state of mind, produced by the work of the last six weeks, and I knew that, come what may, I would be all right. I repeated to myself, "I am releasing myself into perfect health. I am releasing myself into perfect health."

I guess the last sentence about the lines of infection was said aloud, not silently, because with this the technician leaned over and said, "Those are your lymph nodes, not lesions."

"Oh," I said with a sigh, "thank you for telling me." We had no other chance for conversation, however, because Dr. Ernstoff entered the room with the X rays that had been taken six weeks before. He stuck them into the viewer with the strong, deliberate motion that is customary, and we looked at them side by side.

They were a muddle to me, but soon I heard him say, "Oh, look here, this one is considerably smaller than six weeks ago. That's very good." And then, as my eyes focused on the place he was pointing out, I heard Sy and myself saying in unison, "But where is the second one?" "Mmm . . ." he mused, "well, I can see where it was if I look closely, but it has almost disappeared." Sy and I just looked at each other in amazement as the physician continued, "Of course, looking at the other lung, I can see something that might be developing into another spot over here. We have a method of rating change in an X ray like this. If there is a 50 percent decrease in the lesion, we call it a change. Otherwise, we say that no change has occurred. All in all, I would label the results 'no change.' " Shaking his head in a pleased way, he concluded, "This is a perfect time to start therapy, when so many things are going on."

Finally catching our breath, we responded, "No, this is not the time to start therapy, but to wait to see if some natural process is at work, enhanced by the psychological work that we have been doing." He listened and agreed that we would have to talk a bit more. He was very interested and respectful as we told him about our work with the therapy and the visualizations. We told him that we definitely did not want to begin the program that day and asked him to give us a month to determine if further improvement would occur. He told us that it would be impossible to hold my place for that long because the program was in its final stages and other patients deserved a chance. But he told us to go home for two weeks. He assured us that no significant change could occur in that short time, but at least it would give us time to come to our senses about the program. We thanked him and left.

Although it may seem to some that we made a rash decision by refusing the treatment that was offered, remember that this was not a standard treatment. I was to be a subject in a medical experiment with only a 25 percent chance of improvement and no chance at all of a permanent cure. It was a life-extending operation at best, and it involved terrible risks and continual medical monitoring by blood tests and X rays. I would have felt very different had this been a standard medical procedure because I am convinced that the best of all worlds for the cancer patient is a combination of medical and psychological procedures.

My reaction to the news from the hospital was one of relief and cautious pessimism because the possibility of my left lung being involved was still scary. Sy, however, was elated. Before leaving the hospital I called our daughters, and when I got home I called Didi. Despite some concern, I was also relieved and was looking forward to the next two weeks of relative calm. It was wonderful to have this reprieve, the first time that I could relax a bit in a long time, and I slept soundly that evening.

My dreams, however, were strange. I dreamed that a friend's daughter had been sent out by her mother on a task that she did not understand and didn't know how to begin. I told her that she should take it one step at a time. I looked through her pile of papers, picked out one piece, and put it on the top, as if to say, "Here, start with this."

The surface message of this dream was immediately clear to me. It was reflecting the uncertainty that I felt of how to spend the time between examinations—whether to meditate more, what to read, how to think. The basic message was that I should not try to figure out the whole process at one time. Some part of me knew what to do, and it was telling the frantic part of me to calm down and let things happen.

This dream turned out to have a deeper message as well, one that had a profound influence on me at this crucial time in my illness. I had an appointment with Didi that afternoon, and I was surprised when she asked for details of the dream. She was especially interested in my friend's daughter. I immediately began to compare her with my own daughters. This young woman, who was the same age as my daughters, had not been as successful as they in high school. But now she seemed to have it all—a husband, a child, and a well-paying job. By most standards my friend's daughter was more accomplished than either of my daughters, and I was slightly jealous.

Didi stopped me right there. "By whose standards is she more successful than your daughters?" she asked.

I smiled. "By Mickey's standards of course."

"Yes," she said, "by Mickey's standards, brilliant and successful in the world is better. But could you ask for more success than your own daughters, who have shown their tremendous ability to love you and have each helped to save your life?"

I could hardly answer her for the tears in my eyes and the fierce feeling of gratitude that I felt for both of them. I felt so ashamed. This episode showed the power of my Mickey personality, always comparing, always self-critical. I left the therapy session determined above all that Mickey's values had to go.

I fell asleep early that evening. About midnight I awakened, having had a terrible dream that someone was trying to kill me. All during the night the dreams continued. I kept trying to go somewhere, but the road was obscured. I was trying to accomplish something, but the votes kept going against me.

I awakened the next morning feeling very ill at ease. The contents of the dreams were frightening to contemplate. Intuitively, I knew that the dreams had something to do with Mickey. I decided that she had to be abandoned. Her reactions of yesterday and all those that had almost led to my death had to go. With the most determined attitude that I could muster, I started to tell her that she would have to go.

A very clear and powerful image of her immediately

came to mind. I saw her standing in a train station, carrying a little suitcase. She was all alone and I was walking away from her, telling her that she couldn't come with me. She sobbed and sobbed, begging to be taken along. I kept walking, but when I turned to look back the sight of her there all alone was more than I could bear. Suddenly I realized that it was she who was in fear of her life and was calling out in pain. As I now was overwhelmed with emotion, I knew that I could not leave her behind because it was she who contained all my emotions. To live without emotions, even the bad ones, was impossible—I might as well be dead. I turned to her and told her to come, that I was going to take her up the mountain with me once more.

It was not my usual meditation, but a visualization of a trip up the mountain. All of my subpersonalities were there: I held Baby Alice in my arms and I had Little One and Mickey by the hand. Amanda walked with us; Oriole was on my shoulder.

When we got to the ledge where so many important changes had taken place on other trips, I believed that we should all think about letting go and just float off the cliff. But it didn't happen that way. Instead, the builder, Amanda, changed into a flying horse and we all took off with her. It was wonderful to feel the power of her wings as they slowly beat up and down. Then all at once I realized that we could not only fly, but if we caught the circular currents, we could soar like a hawk. We caught the air current and the warm wind wafted us up higher and higher. It was an incredible experience.

As I came out of the visualization I understood why I could not leave Mickey behind: I desperately needed her energy, her intense motivation, and her emotions. Her motivation was all wrong and her energy was misdirected, but she had loved and had given to others, else, how did all the love come back to me? Didi told me that she must change. Now I, too, understood and was ready for her to change. At last I really loved her.

What happens after an experience like this? It was obviously a major step forward, and I knew it. For the first few hours I had a profound sense of unity and emotional release. I was able to relax and enjoy my new integration. But by evening I was again agitated. I think this indicates that any major change, even one that brings a much-desired integration, is unsettling.

That night I again dreamed and dreamed. I was being shown through a large house by the caretaker, who kept in contact with all of the rooms by walkie-talkie. Upstairs the rooms were large and beautifully decorated; downstairs there were small workrooms, each one devoted to a single activity. In the last scene we were all walking down a beautiful staircase when the husband of the house announced proudly, "You are all going to meet a BASTARD." He seemed so pleased to be introducing us to this person.

This dream contained only one clear image for me as I thought about it and free-associated to its main elements. The word *bastard* reminded me of the bastard file that Marty uses to sharpen her skis before a race. I remembered once standing along the side of a giant slalom race course and seeing a young woman rounding the bend going at a furious rate—the fastest of any racer so far. I was shocked to realize that it was Marty, and I both admired her courage and feared for her. So, in general, the dream was telling me to "go for it" but to be careful.

At the time this dream occurred I was surprised at how prosaic it was and how little it reflected the pivotal experience of accepting Mickey. But on the most recent reading of the dream, I realize that I did appreciate how important the integration was and why it had occurred. I believe that the house represented my mind. The caretaker (my therapist) was showing me that my mind had beautiful upper rooms (higher experiences like the one with Mickey and the flying horse) as well as other rooms where ordinary, well-organized experiences took place. Her walkie-talkie gave her the ability to contact all of the spaces at once and was probably a reminder to myself that I could do this too. The bastard was another representation of myself. Some part of me was very proud of my recent accomplishment and was reminding me that I had done it because I had broken with my connections to my birth family and had struck out on my own.

The next day Didi listened to all that had been happening to me with little comment except to say that "Of course you couldn't abandon Mickey, it was impossible; transformation was the only way." She then asked me to search out one more subpersonality, a wise guide. She told me to go up the mountain by myself so that I could find the higher aspects of existence, my transpersonal self. Later that day, when I followed her instructions at home, I met Athena, the Greek goddess of wisdom. She was no longer the immature jealous goddess of the Trojan War days but had turned into an older woman. She lived by the wayside and had an excellent perspective on life. Her wisdom is that she knows that wisdom and happiness come from small things.

Finding Athena was the last step in the process of integration that had begun with my acceptance of Mickey. The peace that I had expected finally came. The next day, during my meditation, a warm feeling began to envelop my heart and my chest. I wanted to bask in the wonderful sensation of calm and unity forever. As I went about my activities for the day, I realized that other people could also see that I was changed. Lisa commented that I looked radiant, and other people who saw me that day all commented on how well I looked. I couldn't see it myself, but I could feel the difference.

This look and this feeling lasted for a few days and then slowly abated, because the world was still out there to deal with. Often during these days I would feel light-headed and dizzy. I became tired from having to talk and interact with my family, but especially I found it difficult dealing with other people's feelings and hurts. Early in the second week of my short reprieve, I discussed the problem of empathy with Didi. She helped me with an exercise to create a space within which no one would be allowed to penetrate. I practiced with her saying "no" to people, and these exercises came in handy as I began to make contact with old acquaintances whom I hadn't seen since my illness. I was beginning a different approach to life. It seemed to be working and I was pleased.

As the day neared for me to return to the hospital, my feeling of euphoria was replaced by a growing feeling of panic. On Tuesday evening of the second week after our trip to New Haven, I had a disturbing dream. Sy, our younger dog Chaya, and I were visiting somewhere and were staying in a hotel. Suddenly I was outside looking back at the hotel. The whole left section of the building was ablaze. I ran into the building to warn Sy and the dog. I awakened yelling, "Fire! Fire!" as loud as I could.

Since I never had anxiety dreams during the really bad times, I assumed that the good news had lifted some of my inhibitions and that my fears about imminent disaster might be coming out. However, in this dream, the danger was not to myself. So I now understand that it also represented my fear that my growing autonomy might lead to a loss of love from Sy. That is, it represented the old conflict over autonomy and relationship.

All too soon that second Monday arrived and we found ourselves once more on the road to New Haven. From the time we reached the outskirts of the city the trip was a disaster. Unlike the two other times that we had visited the hospital, we thought that we knew the way and so we were not paying attention to the signs and missed our first turn. I was driving, and began to feel extremely tense in the unfamiliar surroundings of streets in repair, so I asked Sy to take the wheel. After about five minutes of confusion, we finally began to get our bearings and were able to negotiate our way to the hospital.

Since our appointment was later in the morning than the first time, all of the parking spaces reserved for the hospital were taken and we had to park in the huge parking garage several blocks away. Of course we had trouble finding a parking space and so we were late for our appointment. By this time the waiting room was filled and there was a certain tension in the air that had never been there before. Eventually, however, we were called to the desk and told to go across the street to the X-ray department for another X ray.

Here, too, things were very different from what we had experienced two weeks before: our wait was interminable and the attendants were impatient. We finally got the large envelope with the pictures and returned across the street. By this time my tension was mounting and I foolishly took the envelope into one of the viewing rooms unannounced. They took the X rays and told me they would call me when it was my turn. I walked out into the waiting room once more and started to try to read a magazine. Reading was impossible but I looked at the pictures and tried to calm myself by meditating with my eyes open but directed to the floor.

A half hour passed. Other patients came and went and still they did not call my name. Soon I looked at my watch and realized that an hour had passed since we had returned from across the street. I looked around in the waiting room, and I could see that there were no patients left and some of the assistants were leaving for lunch. As I wondered what we should do next the woman who had examined me at my first intake came out to the desk. I walked up to her and asked when they were going to let me see the results of the new X rays. She looked at me in a puzzled way and said, "What are you still doing here? Didn't he come out to tell you? The growth is much smaller, you can see it without any measurement. I thought by now you had left." I turned away from her so that she couldn't see that I was crying, and I practically collapsed into Sy's arms. I guess I only fall apart when the news is good!

Dr. Ernstoff showed us the X rays, and of course I was disappointed because the change was not as dramatic as I had been led to expect. No matter, it was obvious that there was a change for the better, despite the physician's previous assertion that no discernible difference could occur in such a short period of time. He kept telling us that he still would read the X ray as "no change" officially, but he agreed with us that there was no point in my starting any interferon therapy at the present time. He left us by telling us that we could come back in the future if it was necessary and that there would be new and better programs of all kinds that we could consider. He handed us the envelope with all the pictures in it, wished us good luck, and said good-bye.

We will never know why he kept us waiting so long before telling us such good news. It is Sy's contention that he just didn't know how to handle the information that went so counter to his knowledge and experience. We talked a lot about this strange reaction on the way home as we released the tension of what seemed like a lifetime of waiting in that room. But by the time we got to Hartford we had our minds on the future, not the past, and for the first time since I became ill, the future looked very good. *Perhaps I will grow old with Sy after all,* I thought as I turned my sights to thinking about what I might be doing with the rest of my life.

PART III

Quest for Wholeness

12

Grappling with the Guilt Monster

It was now early June. In just six weeks I had accomplished my major goal: I had turned myself around psychologically and physically and now had a new lease on life. I had absolutely no symptoms and I felt normal. But it is important to point out that in medical terms I was still desperately ill. There was a malignant tumor the size of a large marble in my lung. My physicians believed that this was a temporary remission that could reverse itself at any time. The task ahead was to put the disparate pieces of my personality together into an integrated whole. My life depended on the outcome.

My quest for wholeness was in some ways more difficult than the recent battle against imminent death. The psychological work of the past six weeks was like swimming through shark-infested waters—the only goal was to reach shore alive. Now the real journey was about to begin. The goal was to reach the top of a high and rugged mountain. I had no idea what monsters lay in wait for me, but I believed that I was equal to the task. Although I was eager to begin the next phase of therapy, it was possible to reduce the pace a little. Didi and I decided that I was ready to reduce our sessions to once a week.

Just before I became ill Marty had become engaged. Her plans to be married had been postponed because of my operation, but now she and her fiancé decided on a September wedding. What better way to return to life than to plan Marty and Toby's wedding? The wedding plans also provided me with the first test of my new maturity. Complications that a year ago would have sent me into a tailspin worked out very well because I had learned how to make my wants known and how to make my family respond to my needs in a healthy manner.

During the first few weeks after the good news, my spirits were very high. I was filled with intense feelings of gratitude and experienced a flush of energy that I hadn't had for years. I attended a health salon every day and was overjoyed with the progress I was making with my exercises and the continued gain in weight.

Then, as preparations for the wedding began to come together, I experienced a slight physical setback. Near the end of June I began to feel a strange weakness in my arms and legs. I assumed that I was overdoing my exercises, but when it continued over several weeks it began to distress me. Besides the fear that I felt about the weakness in my muscles, there was a sadness from what I felt was a fall from the wonder and the good feeling following the news about my health. Perhaps it was a sense of not being grounded. During my illness I was "grounded" in my determination to live and in my devotion to my meditation. Then I felt grounded in the simple activities of life that I had never expected to be able to resume. I was further distracted by the preparations for the wedding, but all this finally wore off. What remained was a sense of weakness.

My sister, Ruth, finally found an explanation for my feeling of weakness from her health-club advisor, who said that it was probably a muscle fatigue brought on by improper pacing. She recommended slow return to exercises and a lot of patience. This made sense to me and I learned to live with it. I also learned to use the situation to my advantage. It convinced me that there was something that I had to work on psychologically and the symptom was a good point of takeoff for the work ahead.

The next change was that I became obsessed with the idea that I had been saved for some important work in the world and that I would receive a message about my future direction. The "answer" that I sought never came. Instead, there was a disturbing new complication to be dealt with. After several weeks of dreams that were strange and incomprehensible, a pattern began to emerge. I was becoming fearful and full of guilt: I was fearful of phantoms and guilty about silly areas of neglect. I developed a fear that Stewart was angry with me because I was neglecting my meditation, and that somehow he was causing my weakness. I would not allow my sister to visit because I was afraid that she and Sy would argue and that it would affect me. I was fearful of displeasing Marty with the wedding plans and I was afraid that our relationship would deteriorate, as it had when we planned her first wedding. I felt terribly guilty about our older dog, Hava, who had died several months before while we were away visiting my sister. I began to feel guilty about the fact that she died in the kennel and not at home on her favorite couch.

I began to view the guilt and the fear reaction as an aftershock of a serious trauma. While we're in the trauma many reactions are inhibited, to be released only when the event is over. But though part of my reaction could be accounted for in this way, some of the reaction was particular to me. Why, instead of basking in the happiness of my survival, did my thoughts turn to feelings of guilt? I turned to examine these feelings. Guilt is another form of self-negation. Perhaps it is a little less serious than the self-hatred that was killing me, but their origin is the same.

Didi and I took on my guilt reactions in our weekly sessions. We concentrated on the relationship that I had with my parents in the years after my marriage when they refused to have anything to do with me. In the typical old fashion, I told her that I had made mistakes in my dealing with them over my marriage, but she refused to listen to this. She asked me to contrast our approach to Marty, who also once was about to marry against our better judgment, with the way my parents had treated me. She reminded me that Sy and I agreed to support Marty in her choice even though we thought it was wrong for her. In contrast, my parents disowned me and rejected me completely. She assured me that no matter how poorly I may have handled the situation, their complete rejection of me was uncalled for.

She felt, moreover, that I had forgiven them too easily and had been too eager to make a reconciliation. She believed that at some level I should have faced them with their complicity in rejecting me. In other words, when I realized that my mother was dying of cancer, I completely absolved them of any guilt and returned as the "good daughter" who would not rock the boat. This, she felt, was a mistake and a continuation of my willingness to accept responsibility too easily.

Thinking back to my childhood, I realized that I had always felt guilty for everything bad that happened, and that it may have started at the time of the death of my mother's twelve-year-old brother, Teddy. It would not be unreasonable for my grandmother to have resented my presence when she had just lost her adored son. As a result I may have been psychologically primed to assume responsibility not only for Teddy's death but for all the things that went wrong.

It seemed strange to think in these terms, because to an outsider I was the family member who seemed to get all the praise and admiration. But I was also the one who was programmed to be different, and so, when I challenged the family values by marrying Sy, it was easy to sacrifice me on the alter of family unity. Then, when it was time for me to be allowed back in once more, it was on the terms that we never discuss the issue again. It was very helpful for me to express these ideas, but it didn't make me feel better for long.

Sy and I started to take a more direct approach to the puzzle of my terrible guilt feelings by visualizations. I sat quietly for a few minutes with my eyes closed. Then I began to concentrate on the word *guilt.* I heard a gavel pounding on a desk and the words *I pronounce you guilty.* Suddenly I saw myself at the time of Teddy's death. I was in my grandmother's kitchen, asking for a drink of water. My grandmother sat with her head in her hands, looking very depressed. She turned to my mother and said, "Why did you bring her with you? This is no place for her now." I felt terribly sad and confused as I came out of the session, but connecting the feeling to the incident helped to assuage my psychological discomfort for a while.

The next day I tried another approach. As Didi had suggested several times with other events and feelings, I tried to find out who among my subpersonalities was hurt by my grandmother and the events associated with Teddy's death and what was needed to make things right. I closed my eyes and tried to regain the feeling that I had as a child. A very clear and pathetic image came to mind. There was Baby Alice pulling a huge wagon filled with hay. This was not a toy wagon but a real old-fashioned farmer's wagon full of hay. It was almost impossible for her to budge the thing, but she was pulling and tugging at it and crying.

I realized immediately that it was she who was not only the most frightened of my subpersonalities but the one who had the longest list of wrongs to be righted. This was the key I needed. Baby Alice had to be able to verbalize all of the insults and wrongs done to her and then to forgive them. The list was practically inexhaustible, as indicated by the size of the wagon, and it took days for all the hurt to come out. She was especially angry at Nana, and even more so at my mother for not protecting her against Nana. That seemed to be her most telling indictment—that she had not been protected by her parents and by the other subpersonalities. After several days of ranting and raving about these indignities, she placed herself in a throne room and received an apology from each of the subpersonalities. She, in turn, forgave them, but only after their assuring her that they would never let it happen again.

As this exorcism of old injustice proceeded I developed a sense of calm and wonder as I began to taste what life would be like without feeling that heavy burden of guilt. The next time I visualized Baby Alice she appeared all dressed up and pulling a little red toy wagon. The hay wagon never appeared again.

I decided that I should try to elevate this personality to her highest level. So I took her up the mountain with the red wagon and she threw it off of the ridge. It turned into a beautiful sailboat and I thought we were rid of it for good. Much to my surprise, however, this was only a temporary transformation of the wagon. Baby Alice did not figure in my therapy for several weeks after the trip up the mountain. But when she appeared again the wagon was still with her. This vehicle was a mysterious symbol associated with the Baby Alice personality. Understanding what it meant to her became a most important part of therapy and played a significant role in the development of this frightened child into an assertive person.

In the next few weeks after the breakthrough with Baby Alice, I felt well and less tense than I had before. The wedding preparations continued and gave me something to occupy my time. We selected a photographer, a caterer, a florist, a band, and we had all the bridesmaids organized and their dresses were in the process of being made. We had also met Toby's parents for the first time. I was a little quiet on our first meeting, since extended social interaction out of my family or close friends was still a little difficult for me, but I liked Toby's father and was especially impressed with Toby's mother, who was a beautiful and gracious lady.

With all of the plans for the wedding in order for the time being, I could return to my meditation and to new avenues in my therapy. I should have known that I was far from finished with my feelings of guilt, because self-negation was the most common way that I had reacted to the world. By working with Mickey's intense self-hatred, and Baby Alice's general feeling of being bad, I had begun the healing of my self-negation at its core. The next phase was to deal with the sensitivities and compulsions that had rippled out from these feelings to my relationships with specific people.

While the world saw me as a nice person because I was so understanding of people with trouble, I was miserable because I couldn't separate myself from the feelings of others. This reaction was especially true with respect to my sister, Ruth. When something bad happened to her I always felt that it was my special responsibility to give her something to make up for her discomfort. Undoubtedly this was caused by the unassuaged rage that I felt at her birth and was undoubtedly part of the baggage that Baby Alice carried around in the original hay wagon. While I had calmed Baby Alice's general feeling of being bad, there were still the secondary reactions, such as those to my sister, that had to be worked out.

In retrospect I can identify a spiral movement of healing that worked back and forth from the general to the specific and back again. I began in the abstract, with vague dreams that left a mood of fear and remorse several weeks after I knew that I would live. The general mood was soon translated into specific and unreasonable fears about Stewart, Ruth, and Marty. Then, through fantasy, I discovered a general feeling of being bad that was calmed via my work with Baby Alice. Soon, however, I was back to the specific as the process continued on another level with another subpersonality.

I am convinced that I was looking for a specific issue to deal with, and if one had not occurred, I would have created one. As it happened my sister provided me with an excellent cause. In one of our weekly telephone conversations about plans for Marty's wedding, I discovered that I may have inadvertently disappointed her when she was married by not giving her a shower. It is a long story, and there were good reasons involved, but the main point is that I felt terrible when I made this discovery. She was not accusing me of any failure, but from what she said I *deduced* that I may have hurt her a great deal. That started a new wave of remorse and concern on my part about what I should do now. I wanted to call her and beg her forgiveness, but even in my distraught state I intuitively knew that I should wait until I talked it over with Didi.

In therapy I discussed with Didi how much Ruth must feel my lack of authenticity when I interact with her, and how much my protective attitude toward her must infuriate her. She is also very sensitive to our basic disagreement on many issues, including politics. She may well be angered by my projection of a lack of respect for her ideas. I have the feeling that she and I are often trying to prove ourselves to each other. That cannot be the basis for a very good relationship. Didi sensed that this was an important issue for me to resolve and asked me if I would try to visualize saying good-bye to my sister. She told me that, after all, if the relationship was hurting me, I didn't have to continue it. I told her that I knew this but that I loved my sister and cherished the relationship we had. I wanted to work it out if I could.

The visualization of saying good-bye to Ruth was very hard for me to do because after I said good-bye I kept looking back. Even with Didi's prompting, I couldn't really say good-bye. She concluded that I wasn't really ready yet and that to continue would do no good. However, we talked about the concept of looking back. Somehow, with Ruth, the concept of looking back was not only continuing a connection but also continuing a comparison. With Ruth I am always comparing and judging my own position with respect to her and to the standards of others. Unfortunately, we didn't ever finish this attempt to deal with my sister. But in other ways we did come back to the subject and made some resolution of it.

Marty came for a visit one weekend shortly after the therapy session above, and soon my concerns about my sister were forgotten in my concern for her. Now that the arrangements for the wedding were in order, her thoughts were turning to the many responsibilities of her future life. She was unsure of her coming role as stepmother to two teenaged children and was insecure about Toby's growing desire to sell his business and start something new. I assured her that she and Toby had a lot going for them and that they could work out any problems that came along. Although she seemed calmer when she left, I began to worry about her and to feel slightly guilty that somehow I had not taken her fears seriously enough.

During my next therapy session Didi suggested that we visualize what all this worrying meant to me. I tried to find an image that represented the feeling of guilt. What I saw was a scene at a jousting match: an open field surrounded by trees and stands for the spectators. Marty and Ruth and Nana were sitting in the stands. Farther on was a huge tree to which I was tied with large coils of rope. Nana had shot a small arrow attached to a long silken thread into my heart. My subpersonality Little One was standing in front of me with her mask on and crouched over. In her hand was the other end of the thread, which she was moving in response to subtle instructions from the princesses.

Every time Little One moved the thread a shot of pain surged through my chest. I could control the pain somewhat by taking up the slack in the thread and lessening the impact. I also had the feeling that I could exorcise the arrow by pulling it out myself. I knew, however, that it was a barbed arrow and would have to be pushed in and twisted in order to get it out.

Didi and I had not had much time to analyze the visualization so its impact stayed with me and I remained in a state of distress. A day later I was still suffering from the effects of the imaginary arrow in my chest. At one point I became very dramatic with Sy and "threatened to pull the splinter out myself" if that was what was needed to rid me of this horrible feeling. Sy and I talked about what I got out of this feeling, why I seemed to nurture it. He assumed that somehow it must make me feel superior or give me control of some other emotion that might be worse if it were released. From other conversations we had had in the past, I knew he believed the guilt that I was feeling was the inhibitor of some intense hostility that I would eventually have to express. But we did not discuss this aspect of the issue at the time. Instead, together we listed my "crimes" that had been brought out recently and that had caused me such pain. We decided they were crimes of passion or omission more than premeditated wrongs, and that regret was a more appropriate reaction than this intense guilt that I was feeling.

He asked me why I thought it was Little One at the other end of the thread. Why was Little One angry with me? I told him that, unlike Mickey, she knows I love and admire her but do not respect her. Perhaps the worst part is that she is separated from the other subpersonalities and from the world. Her mask is one form of separation, and the fact that she has an animal form as well as a human form is another way she is different from the other subpersonalities. That is probably why she does not get along with the others and why she is mean to them. This talk calmed me down for a while but it did not settle the issue.

The next week Didi and I continued on the same subject. We approached the issue in the way that we had handled things before by asking what Little One wanted. I told Didi that she wants recognition of her viewpoint, her needs, and most of all she wants to be incorporated not separated from me. She knows that I love her and admire her at some level, but she is unbridled passion and I shy away from that.

Didi told me that she believes Little One to be an undeveloped two-and-a-half-year-old child. At this stage I have not developed my sense of self and space and so there is no rational control over her feelings. They are a source of guilt because they must be satisfied and sometimes lead to dire consequences. My greatest sense of guilt in this respect was that the day before Lisa and her twin were born, I moved heavy furniture myself because I was too impatient to wait for Sy to help me. They were born two months early and the first baby died.

Didi went on to say that this subpersonality needs to be integrated. She is a product of my confusion at a very crucial time, probably at the death of my uncle Teddy. No one explained anything to me and suddenly my world changed. I was swept into an adult world, never again to be the center of attraction and yet I was unable to maturely express my needs and desires. I agreed with much of what Didi was saying, but I didn't know how this would allow the situation to change.

The following morning I hit on an idea that I liked. I would be Little One for the day in order to feel what it was like and to give her the freedom she longed for so much. She liked physical contact, so I played hard with the dog, who had a grand time. I hugged and pushed Sy in fun and I said exactly whatever came to my mind. I had a ball. My theory was that she should have a time to express herself before we talked about that integration word. It was strange because at one level she wanted to be integrated and at another the word was anathema to her. How confusing!

I wrote in my journal that day about how much I loved this part of me and I vowed to assure her of that love. I admitted that she always comes last, last, last . . . and that I would try to change this. By the end of the day I felt much better.

On the next day I decided that it was time to try to get Little One together with my other subpersonalities. Each of them came over to her and acknowledged her legitimacy and her existence. The scene ended with all of us in a huge spaceship surveying my body for cancer. I was not sure if the integration had worked but it was a first step. I wrote in my journal that if I had to become Little One again, I would do it. But it seemed to me that the best approach now was to train her not to assume her identity. I also vowed to do something that she wanted to do every day: go to a baseball game, climb a mountain . . . something.

By the middle of July six more weeks had passed and I had completed the transition from my meditative life to a more normal social existence. It was again time for an X ray, and to the delight of all, we could see continued disappearance of the one remaining lesion.

If I were to summarize my accomplishments in these weeks, the most important would be my newfound confidence in dealing with my family in a self-enhancing way under normal living conditions. Next, I was greatly encouraged by my growing ability to use fantasies with my subpersonalities to identify and defuse strange moods that seemed to come from nowhere. It is interesting to note that the fantasies associated with my subpersonalities were different from the visualizations of myself in light or the Simonton visualization of destroying the cancer cells. The latter were specific states that I was purposely trying to achieve. In other words, I knew what the image was in general, and the only issue was whether I could achieve it or not. With the subpersonalities I was visualizing a feeling or I was asking the personality to help me with some issue. The images that came to mind came freely out of my imagination and then took off into a story line that I did not control.

Since the images came from my subpersonalities, they represented feelings and information that were not available to me in any other form. This is because each subpersonality represented a unified emotional and action potential that existed as a syndrome. I believe that these images were close to the higher self that psychosynthesis talks about. They may not seem to have been higher in terms of their subject matter, but they were higher in their authenticity. By following these fantasies wherever they led, I was giving myself the respect that I needed. I was giving myself a form of unconditional love.

There was something else. By using the fantasies I was allowing each part of myself to proceed at its own pace, to get as much emotional support for change as it needed. I really had no choice but to allow the subpersonalities to proceed as they wished because I never understood or could predict their paths until they were fulfilled. You can see this principle in my premature attempt to elevate Baby Alice before her time. She complied with my naive idea that she needed to get rid of her wagon in order to grow up, but only temporarily. She was not ready to give it up because there were things that she had to do with the wagon that I did not understand. When she was ready the wagon disappeared. But that time was still a long way away.

The third accomplishment was to begin the healing of the area outside of the personality core. The most important work in the first six weeks had been with Mickey and my core of self-hatred. I was still working at the core when I connected the vague feelings of fear and guilt to Baby Alice. But after that I began to reach out to heal the area that affected my interactions with other people. In other words, I began to get at the wider problem of being conditioned too much to the needs and criticisms of others. This process involving Little One brought out the relationship between moods involving fear and guilt and the dominant personality trait of exaggerated concern for others. I knew that other moods would come and that there were other hard days ahead, but I had confidence in the method of identifying the subpersonality that was involved in each particular case.

There was something else happening that was subtle but consistent. In at least three or four cases, I had defused strong feelings without having to spend much time on direct catharsis. Sy had always assumed that I would have to confront my repressed hostility. I assumed that this meant that I would have to pound pillows or yell and scream a lot. This just was not true. By letting Baby Alice and Little One express their feelings via fantasy, there seemed to be no need for anything else. I was beginning to realize that, in my case, the direct expression of emotions was less important than achieving a sense of vindication of my views and gaining assurance from some part of myself that painful situations would not occur again.

In Switzerland I had been very angry at Sy for what I viewed as his special treatment of our friend Georgia. No amount of ranting and raving at him helped. While it helped somewhat for me to try to control the feeling before it reached the point of needing strong expression, this did not address the real problem. Using the examples of my recent therapy, what I needed was to find out how I could get my views to be taken seriously by someone else, and how I could supply myself with the needed love or respect that had eluded me because of my former self-negativity and powerlessness. While I certainly did not have the understanding of the whole process that I do now, I intuitively knew that I could trust my subpersonalities to lead me to eventual psychological health and wholeness.

13

Spirit and Flesh

As the summer of 1985 wore on I entered a period of great discontent. I dealt less with my subpersonalities and more with the underlying themes of spirituality and sensuality and their ramifications in my life. The regression that Sy feared did take place, but its consequences were not as serious as he had anticipated.

The month of August started on a high note with a vacation to the Cape. Sy attended a seminar on immunology and I was free in the morning to enjoy the magnificent beaches at Eastham. Together, we played tennis, walked and swam at the beach, and ate dinner out. It was a fine place to rest and find a sense of renewal.

Part of the fun of vacations was the break in the usual routine and the chance for Sy and me to concentrate on ourselves, both emotionally and sexually. I had gone through all kinds of moods with respect to sex in the past four months. Right after returning home from the hospital, I delighted in the physical togetherness and joy of sexuality. It was a wonderful life-enhancing experience at a time of physical discomfort and fear. But as my condition worsened and I faced the possibility of imminent death, my sexual desires became secondary to the need for disciplined meditation. I desired separation and autonomy more than sexuality, although I strongly needed to be held and comforted.

Now that I faced the chance of a longer life, I wanted to express my joy in living in all ways. But somehow this didn't happen in the way that I had expected. Somehow I still felt the inhibition of those earlier months and I couldn't understand why. Little One, the dancer, who expresses all of my emotions in the most straightforward and open way, had told me once that I was afraid to be completely well for fear of letting loose her full sexual potential. I thought about her statement sometimes when I was alone on vacation, but I thought I could bypass dealing with the issue.

About three days into the vacation I knew that the problem was not going to be solved just by being away. The first indication came when my lips began to swell with severe fever blisters. It had been years since I had such an outbreak, although as a young girl they were common to me in periods of extreme tension. I attributed the symptom to the fact that I had stayed in the sun too long. But in my heart I knew that it was a message that something was wrong. I recalled that the last severe outbreak had been the day that I first told my parents that I wanted to marry Sy. I was particularly upset that day at my father's reaction, and I accepted the fact that this symptom now meant that I was not ready for a complete release of sexuality until I had worked out the remaining issues with him. And what a perfect symptom, guaranteed to act as an inhibitor and to express the basic issue that I somehow felt dirty and guilty about my sexuality.

My dreams gave me the same message. The first night after I realized what was going on, I dreamed about having sex with Sy but being covered with black bugs that wouldn't go away. I tried to collect them on my arm so that I could kill them with one sweep of my hand against the window, but when I got my hand in place they suddenly all died. But then as I threw the dead ones down, a new swarm took their place.

The dream was transparent to Sy and to me. The black bugs, like the blisters on my lips, prevented me from enjoying sex. Both symbols represented guilt about my sexuality—guilt most likely connected to my feelings about my father. We recalled the early years of our marriage when I would awaken in the middle of the night calling for my father. We talked about my feeling that I was betraying my father when I married Sy. We knew that the guilt probably went deeper than that—deeper into my sexual feelings for my father as well. However, this topic had always been a difficult subject for Sy and me to discuss. Although we tried, we made little headway on finding connections between the old feelings and my present concerns about sex.

In my quiet hours alone at the Cape I thought some more about my relationship not only with my father but with Sy as well. I realized that Sy and I were in an important transition period that was affecting our interactions in all ways. There was a purity about all of my relationships in the shadow of death that was not maintained afterward. All of my contacts were on good behavior when they realized I was so sick, and I of course was dealing on the highest spiritual plane. With the imminence of my death pushed into the background, everyone's behavior slipped back into more normal gear. The feeling of normalcy felt awfully good to me, but individual moments of adjustment were often painful. In very subtle ways Sy began to be less involved with my every need and reverted to his more casual ways. On my part I was challenging many of our old ways of relating, making them better in the end but changing the status quo. I think all of this was having an impact on our sexual adjustment, as it was on all phases of our life.

As was my habit when things in the real world became too much for me to handle, I decided to return to a stricter meditation schedule. Throughout these past weeks I had often become distressed that I was neglecting my spiritual path. Both Stewart and Didi had warned me about the possible dire consequences of this and had angered me somewhat by their concerns. But now the need came from me and I honored it. I had brought along a book to read that Anna had sent me several weeks before. I had confided in her that I needed to understand more what had happened to me and how I was curing myself. The book was by Eric Butterworth and was called *Discover the Power Within You.* The basic message was that if we read the New Testament carefully, we will realize that Jesus's real message was that we all have the power to heal within us.

After reading the book I felt somewhat relieved to know that what had happened to me was not that unusual. I became interested in reading the New Testament, which in the past I had never enjoyed. I even tried to go to church again, but the results were the same as before. Formal religion is not for me. However, when I returned to Amherst I joined a small Bible study group that I continue to enjoy to this day. The vacation did get me back to part of my meditation routine and this always was a positive force in my life with or without the threat of illness.

Stewart and Julie lived in our house while we were away and took care of our dog, Chaya. They stayed on after our return for a short visit. I told Stew about my new interest in the Bible and we talked about spiritual things. Somehow the topic turned to his training in the teachings of the guru Yogananda and how he came to believe in God. He ended by telling me that he sees God as pure love and that basically all God asks of anyone is that they love Him as He loves all of us. This simple message reached me and I was determined to try to do what Stew suggested, to extend my love to God.

On the day after Stew and Julie returned to New York, I took time for a special meditation, time when I knew that no one would bother me. I went through all of the usual healing images and then the part of watching my breath. I didn't try to visualize anything in particular but kept thinking of that day when I had used the concept of the astral self that was connected to the universe. I ended this time by extending myself to the universal and giving first thanks and then love as best I could. I was not prepared for the result, which was that I was immediately filled with a sense of overwhelming love that I had never experienced before. There were no images, but the meditation state seemed to fill my whole being with an emotional intensity that was overpowering. The afterglow of what had happened stayed with me for many hours. I have tried to repeat the experience a few times since, but to no avail.

I remained in a spiritual mood for several days, and the feeling that I had some special destiny became very strong again. I toyed with the idea that I was to be a healer, now that I had done some healing on myself. But as time passed I decided that direct healing would never be one of my talents. If I were to have an influence on anyone, it would have to be by my example, not by my direct intervention. When no other great insight or dramatic experience occurred to point my way to the future, I turned once more to psychosynthesis in an attempt to find some new direction.

Didi, as always, had some answers and ideas. First of all she told me that my vacillation lately between concerns about sexuality and spirituality followed insights by Carl Jung on the connection between these basic human needs. "Concern about sexuality often masks a more basic interest in things of the spirit," she said, "and it works the other way too." So she thought that it was quite natural that I had been concerned about both of these subjects just recently.

By the end of the first week after our return, the effect of the vacation had worn off and the euphoria of the wonderful spiritual experience of giving my love to God had abated so that I was left with an amorphous feeling of agitation. The only thing that pulled me back from my growing unhappiness was dealing in the real world with the rest of the preparations for the wedding. Marty came by herself for a few days to keep some appointments and to help me find a dress for the wedding. We were unsuccessful in finding a dress, but I enjoyed the time that I spent with her. At the end of the weekend we all went to a shower for Marty in Cheshire.

Marty's shower was a strain on me. I was not ready for the intrigue of trying to keep the party a secret or for meeting so many new people. I felt unattractive and out of place and spent the whole time sitting in a corner, talking only to those around me. I felt especially inadequate in comparison to Toby's mother, who looked so beautiful and moved so graciously among all of the guests. I became terribly jealous of her.

It was right after the shower that I became sick. On the next morning I awakened ready to meditate, but as soon as I got up I knew that this would not be possible. I had a headache and felt nauseated. I ate sparingly and spent the day resting and reading. I expected to feel better the following day, but it was just as bad on Tuesday as on Monday. A call to my sister gave me assurances of a sort in that everyone in her household had been sick, too, with stomach ailments of one sort or another. We assumed it was the food at the shower. On Wednesday I was worse, not better, and by this time I was beginning to feel weak as well as sick.

As my sister's family began to recover from their ailments

and I didn't, I began to suspect that the real trouble was psychological, not physical, and I tried working with my subpersonalities. I gathered all of them around me to see what was the matter. There were only three of them who wanted to join in the discussion: Mickey, Baby Alice, and Little One. Mickey and Little One were having a fight over my father, mainly over their view of him and what he was like. All of a sudden they were in a large room with my father's coffin in the middle. Little One at first was dancing around the coffin while the other two were looking on. Then suddenly Little One jumped inside the coffin and was yelling that she didn't want them to close the lid. By this time she was doubled up, holding her stomach in pain, as if the experience was having a strong emotional and physical effect on her. Mickey grabbed her and dragged her screaming out of the coffin. In the struggle Little One scraped her side on a jagged metal edge of the coffin and was seriously hurt. As she lay bleeding on the floor she changed into Bagera, the tiger, and it seemed as if she was mortally wounded. Mickey just stood there stunned and in disbelief because she didn't understand how she had hurt her so seriously. But Baby Alice ran into the woods to get some healing herbs, and the last that I saw of them all, Baby Alice was pulling the tiger away in her wagon. Bagera was sitting up and I could see that she was fine. I, on the other hand, was left with an awful feeling and a sense of confusion. None of this helped my physical condition much either.

The next day, fortunately, was my scheduled therapy session and I hoped that Didi would help me out of the problems that I had been having. To my surprise and annoyance, she would not deal with any of the issues and told me that she wanted me to come away from my subpersonalities and concentrate instead on my higher self, on my love for Sy, my gratitude to God, and whatever other manifestations I could think of on the same plane.

I had trouble responding to her request. Finally she asked me to concentrate on just being Alice. "What do you see when you think of Alice?" she asked me.

I told her that I could see a stage on which *The Magic Flute* was being performed. She then asked me to be the author and to change the plot as I wished. I said that the mother must be vindicated and the daughter must choose freely—not be given to the hero by the father. She promised me that we would work on this the next time, but for the time being it was important for me to stop trying so hard and to just let things happen. "All things are transient, Alice," she said. I left with a strange ringing in my ears, but I felt somewhat better.

The next morning I awakened feeling very weak and still very nauseated. By this time I was a wreck emotionally in that I was convinced that the feelings of nausea were caused by more than just the food I had eaten at the shower. Despite the fact that just a month before the X ray of my chest had shown continuous decrease in the lung lesion, I was now sure that my present problem was due to further complications at the site of the original operation in my kidney. Fortunately I was able to reach my physician, who examined me and told me that he saw no cause to be concerned. He gave me a tranquilizer for my stomach and other remedies for acidity. With the first pill I consumed the nausea that I had experienced for over ten days disappeared, and within a few days I was fine again.

My rapid recovery convinced me that the original physical problem had been exacerbated by emotional problems associated with the shower, especially my jealousy of Toby's mother, and perhaps by the discussions about sexuality that began on our trip to the Cape. Although Didi did not want me to discuss the conflict between my subpersonalities over my father, I could not put it aside. I assumed that the events of the past few weeks were stirring up some of the darkest emotions and that it was sending me into a tailspin.

I never found out what Mickey and Little One disagreed about in their view of my father, but I knew that Little One's integration would not be complete until I resolved it. It was pretty obvious to me that Little One had some very strong attachments to my father sexually, and I guessed that Mickey was trying to make her control them. I was heartened by the fact that some good resolution had taken place. Mickey was the clear victor, so her views would prevail. Although it was a severe blow to Little One to accept this resolution, she would live.

I was heartened and surprised by the role that Baby Alice had played in the story. This was the first indication that she possessed healing abilities, and the first time that she acted as a mediator between two of the other subpersonalities. It was also good to see that she and Little One had become close friends, especially when Little One was in her form as Bagera the tiger. Once before these two had shown an affinity for each other when Little One first changed into Bagera and gave Baby Alice a ride on his back.

Thinking about the scene from *The Magic Flute* that resulted from Didi's redirection of my therapeutic efforts, I was amused to realize that I was expressing the same issue from two different perspectives. The fight between Mickey and Little One emphasized the negative, conflict-laden aspect of the message; the scene from *The Magic Flute* took a higher, more positive view. The lesson was the same: I needed to break the tie to my father in order to be complete as a woman.

As the wedding plans progressed and there remained only one week before the ceremony, I felt much better. But the business with my father was still on my mind. A few days later I had a series of dreams that were strange in their content and that I could not understand.

The first dream was sexual in nature and was about a baby whose paternity was a mystery. The second dream was about Marty, who came in and said that someone called and would deliver a turkey. Suddenly the dream changed locale and I was in a dentist's office going through his files for some information about myself. I discovered, however, that the office was nothing but a front—that there was actually no one there.

As I started to relate the dreams to Didi, I began to laugh because suddenly their meaning became very clear. The idea of mysterious paternity and the delivery of a "turkey" could refer to only one thing, my sister's birth. I told Didi that the event had come as a complete surprise to my parents (don't ask me how), to the neighbors, and certainly to me. This was the final blow for me during those crucial months surrounding my sixth birthday when my grandmother was dying of cancer. Out of nowhere a sibling appeared and my life was changed forever. But even more important, I knew that somehow my father was connected to this event as well as my mother.

I did not understand about sex; I did not know how babies were created. But I remember that there were jokes and conversations in the house, veiled allusions to my parents' sexuality that made me understand that there was a connection between my father and this baby. I remember being disgusted by the sight of my mother breast-feeding the baby. My only other memory was of the times when we took the nurse home from the daytime shift. My father would gather me and all the neighborhood children in the car, and after delivering the nurse home, we all went for ice cream. I know that my father represented the only stability for me in a very confused world. If I felt any resentment toward him over his role in my sister's birth, it was one of the many things that I chose to forget. Perhaps some part of me, however, remembered. Perhaps that was also part of the argument between the two subpersonalities that I described above.

Didi and I turned from the time of my sister's birth to other aspects of my close attachment to my father. I told her that, as an adolescent, I often slept with him. For several years after my grandmother died and my sister was born, my mother's father occupied the spare room in the house. But after he remarried my parents stopped sleeping together and each had his/her own room. I heard my mother tell someone once that it was their way of guaranteeing that they would have no more children. This arrangement meant nothing to me as a child, but as an adult I realized that when they took separate rooms, they literally stopped engaging in sexual intercourse. Now, remembering these times, I wondered whether this became a sexually frustrating situation for my father and whether some of these frustrations were manifested in his sleep while I was in bed with him.

As a young child of eight to twelve years old, I would often awaken in the middle of the night and have trouble going back to sleep. If I got up to use the bathroom at these times, I had to pass my father's room on the way back to my own room, and if he was awake, I would ask if I could sleep with him. Although it began as an irregular occurrence, at one period it was common for me to end up in bed with my father and my sister with my mother before the night was over. In our house the doors to our bedrooms were always kept open and these sleeping arrangements were known by everyone and accepted as normal by the whole family. My memories of this time in my life are all pleasant ones. I liked sleeping with my father and I felt secure and special when I did. I have no memory of anything that was sexual in nature between my father and me: he was a warm and loving man and his behavior was quite asexual in general. And yet, as a grown woman, I wondered if while sleeping he had ever made sexual advances to me.

The other part of the dream about the dentist's office remained a mystery to me for a few days, but Sy and I continued to discuss the dream. We talked about the many stories that Freud's patients had told about sexual encounters with their fathers and how he had finally concluded that they were in the imagination and the "desires of the women" and not in reality. But both of us were also fully aware that with the new statistics about incest, many of these stories might be true. We weren't so concerned about finding out what really happened as finding out what my ideas about it were. He asked me to visualize a story about a father and daughter, but I was not too successful. I told some tale about a girl and her father and a panther. The father tried to help her in some way to get out of some problematic situation but he failed to do so. Afterward they never discussed the situation.

Now this story could be interpreted in several ways. It could indicate some secret that the father and the daughter shared about sex. Or it could stand for a more important event that separated my father and me, namely his reasons for not standing up for me when I was married. As I have indicated before, my marriage to Sy took place under very unhappy circumstances. We were both away from home at the University of Wisconsin. I knew that my parents were opposed to our marriage, ostensibly because Sy was Jewish, but also because they felt that he had undue influence over me. I had promised to try to see other men and had agreed not to marry Sy. This arrangement worked for a while, but eventually we got back together and decided to get married.

I wrote a long letter to my parents telling them of my decision and trying to justify it. After waiting a few days for some kind of response, I called them on the telephone. For days and days I tried to contact them at home but they would not answer the phone. After a particularly frustrating weekend, I decided to call my father at the bank on Monday morning. Of course he had to take the call, thinking it was for business, but his voice was cold as ice when he recognized my voice. I told him that I was disturbed about not hearing from them and that I was most surprised about his reaction. I had expected my mother to be very distressed, but I thought he would understand. He told me that I was incorrect in this, and that the whole family felt the same way and didn't want to talk to me. As I hung up the phone I started to tremble and cry in an uncontrollable manner. I was distressed for days, but I decided that it would do no good to try to approach them again. So Sy and I were married and spent the first four years of our married life in complete alienation from my family.

To the day he died my father and I never said a word about that incident, but it was the source of a subtle hurt between us that never healed. After the rift between my family and me was finally patched up because my mother knew she was dying, my mother simply said that this part of our lives was over and we would not ever talk about it again. Perhaps this is not an ideal way to handle the situation, but it was consistent with her past behavior and at least it was her way of acknowledging that it had occurred. For me it was an acceptable end to a painful part of our relationship.

With my father and me, however, there was not even this meager attempt at some kind of completion to the incident.

Because we never tried to deal with it, there remained a strong sense on my part that he had let me down. I suppose he may have felt the same. The sum total of the experience was that we reestablished a loving relationship with each other, but for me it was never the same.

With these associations aroused by the dream about the dentist, I knew that I had a lot of work before me concerning my relationship to my father, but I was not sure how I should proceed. I spent many days thinking about how I could let go of this feeling of resentment. Lisa had given me a tape on forgiveness that I took out again and used with my father in mind. I worked hard on the forgiveness tapes, but to no avail.

I then turned once again to my notes on the fight between Mickey and Little One. Maybe there was more to it than I had at first believed. By physically pulling Little One away from the coffin, Mickey may have been trying to convince Little One to give up a sensual relationship with my father that was destructive to her. The part of my recent dream about the dentist came to mind. What might it be trying to tell me? I concentrated on the part about the search for something concerning myself in the dentist's office—that is, in the office that was a fake. Looking carefully into the meaning of the dentist to me, I concluded that it was a double symbol: it represented my father because he often took me to the dentist when I was young and, in general, a dentist represents a painful experience. I reasoned that the dream was telling me that it was a waste of time to search in my past for sexual memories of my father and me—to dig up all the pain that it might entail. After all, the dentist's office was a sham, a facade, it had no substance to it. If this was true, then both the dream and the visualization had the same message: Come away from the idea of a real sexual tie with your father. Instead, the best assumption I could make was that the real desire for a special relationship with my father was on my part, not on his, so the pain was of my own making.

I felt that the dream could be interpreted in a broader way too. That is, it was telling me to come away from the idea that others had made my problems, and that instead I should look to my own complicity in my situation. The main issue was not that I lacked special relationships, but that I consistently gave away my autonomy. I felt a strong need to regain control over my life. At least this was the best understanding of what my inner wisdom was telling me, and I became receptive to believing in it at last.

One final bit of information supported the idea that I should try to pull myself out of the emotional mire that I had sunk into in the past few weeks. At this time I went for another chest X ray, and to my dismay, there was no discernible improvement. True, there was no regression either, but I was used to the idea that the lesion was slowly disappearing. I was determined to stop the period of backsliding associated with the emotional and physical strain concerning the wedding and the feelings of turmoil surrounding the work I was doing with my father. It was time to get on with my complete recovery.

14

Looking for Baby Alice

Marty and Toby were married in September 1985. We were happy about the marriage because, in contrast to her choice of two years before, her husband-to-be seemed perfect for her.

The wedding was a great success. The rainy weather broke into glorious sunshine in time for the outside ceremony; none of the bridesmaids tripped on the stone steps during the procession; the food was wonderful; and a week before the wedding I found the perfect dress to wear. Marty was a beautiful bride, not only in her physical appearance, but in the inner calm and maturity she showed as her wedding day arrived. I must admit that I was not as calm as I wanted to be, but I was so grateful to have lived to see her married that I accepted my small periods of tension with amazing equanimity. Her wedding was a great accomplishment for all of us.

The wedding was also a watershed in my journey to health. In the six months before the wedding I was engaged in a struggle against illness and inner turmoil. I had always been good at overcoming adversity, and my success so far proved it. However, in the months that followed, my task was to find a rewarding direction for the rest of my life. I had failed miserably in this respect, and I knew that I had one last chance. I was now poised at the crest of a mountain, searching for my path with heart.

At first I made no major commitment. Instead, I moved into a holding pattern by volunteering time to the League of Women Voters, the Red Cross Blood Bank, and the Audubon Society Sanctuary. I became very tired and somewhat disoriented with the sheer stimulation of these new interactions. Didi helped me with the problem of other people "intruding" on me psychologically by teaching me little tricks to reduce the impact from the outside. I used this method when telephone conversations became too stimulating. Sy would see me moving my hand away from my body as if pushing some unseen force. It worked for me until I got used to being in the outside world and began to enjoy all the activity.

I felt well physically and had no major mood swings at this time. The issue of sexuality seemed to fade into the background after I decided not to try to dig up old memories of my father and me. Sometimes I enjoyed sex very much and acted as freely as I had in the past, and sometimes I didn't. But I was more accepting of my reaction now; I was more tolerant of myself. I wanted the next X ray of my chest to show more progress, so I vowed to pay more attention to my meditation and to therapy.

However, as the weeks passed, I became bored and agitated about my lack of direction. I noticed that my dreams began to show signs of anxiety again. There were dreams of balloons out of control and escalators running amuck and crashing. In thinking about the dreams, I associated the fact of being up high with my concern about my changing status in the world. My first concern was with my short-term status. Was I going to get completely well or would my future be always indefinite? Sy was already referring to my condition as a miracle, yet there was the one small lesion that had not gone away.

Beyond my immediate health there was the nagging question of what I would do with myself if my recovery continued. What would I do with the rest of my life? Sometimes that latter question was more anxiety-producing than the former. I felt that I was well but not yet thriving, and that my eventual longevity would depend on whether I could move ahead, not just stand still. The most important issue was whether I could find some work that would please me and use my talents.

Then one night I had an anxiety dream that sent me on to new paths that I needed to tread. As always, I followed my destiny wherever my dream messages led. I fell asleep immediately on retiring and began to dream. Within an hour I awakened in terror.

In the dream a young woman and I were walking along a dark lonely street. She had a small flashlight to show us the way, but the road became more and more frightening as we progressed. Suddenly I heard a motorcycle rev up in the distance and start to approach us. Instinctively we knew that it was menacing to us, so we hid under a porch. Strangely enough, my friend kept the flashlight on despite the fact that I begged her to shut it off. The cyclist passed by at first, but the light attracted him and he stopped and turned around. He was starting back for us when I woke up. I awakened with a strong sense of malevolence around me.

The next day I discussed the dream with Didi, who interpreted it as being about my need to "shine." Like anyone else, I like to do things well, to be appreciated and praised. But there has always been a catch, always someone who was disturbed by my success, always the other kids who did worse. There was also the picture of besting my sister. None of this was new, but what was new was the sense of hostility and evil that accompanied the light being shone by someone in the dream.

I associated that feeling with my present concern with a friend who had been most helpful to me during my illness but who wanted to retain the old relationship and was becoming annoyed with me as I got better. This person was disturbed that I was shining and wanted to take off on my own. I understood the full message of the dream: In order to get well and find my path in life, I had to get over the fear that I would evoke malevolence on myself from others if I was successful.

The fear of success was along the spectrum of self-hatred that I had begun to reverse. The original problem was at the most negative end of this continuum. It represented an impediment of self-hatred that had to be removed in order for me to stay alive. Now, in order to move ahead, I had to overcome the fear of bringing down the wrath of others on me. I had to overcome my fear of success.

Didi and I talked about the feeling that had been evoked by the dream and by my friend. I told her that it was terrifying because it contained a threat of supernatural powers that could reach out beyond a person's physical presence. Didi assured me that she didn't believe that anyone would do me any harm. But she asked me to tell her about other people whom I believed had this same power. When I named my mother her interest really peaked. "Tell me about your mother," she said. "Why haven't you told me this before?"

I told her that my mother had many strange ways that I never understood, such as trying to contact her dead mother through a medium for several years after her death. There were other things about my mother that gave her an otherworldly aura. She had an uncanny way of knowing things about my thoughts and my behavior that no one else knew.

It was very difficult for me to tell even the most innocent white lie to her as a result. For these reasons it didn't surprise me that I had a strange experience with her when she died. It was just six months from the time that my family and I had finally reconciled that my mother died. Sy and I were living in Wisconsin at the time and I was devastated to learn of her illness shortly after my reunion with her. As she became progressively more ill, I went home for two months to help take care of her. In May I decided that I had to return to spend some time with Sy. Soon after my return, however, my father called and told me that I should come home again if I wanted to see her alive. I planned to go in a day or two. The next night I was awakened in the middle of the night by a knocking at the door of our little prefabricated house. I had a strong image of my mother at the door, but I was too terrified to get up and let her in. The next morning, when my father called to tell me that she had died during the night, I told him that I knew. To this day I feel disappointed with myself for my cowardice, but I know that she understands.

What was good about our discussion was that it led once more to a strong feeling of love for my mother very similar to what I had experienced in the first days of therapy. I recalled how much I shared with her, how much we were alike in our abilities. I began to appreciate that if I somehow had learned to heal myself, it may have been through some inborn abilities that I had inherited from her. A fantastic sense of love for her ensued in my meditations later that evening. I made a point of asking her to continue to help me and I told her how much I loved her and appreciated the gifts that she had given me.

That night I had a dream I did not understand at first and that led to a memory I could find no connection for. I was on a muddy road with Sy and I indicated that we must go around not straight through. Then the dream switched to a scene in a school: my mother was with me, and I was applying for admission. There was a man in the dream who I thought was a staff member, but who turned out to be a student. We were in the cafeteria teasing him. He spilled his milk as a result of our actions and we laughed at the fact that we were causing him so much grief.

On awakening I still did not understand the dream, but suddenly I knew why Baby Alice always had her wagon with her. A strong image flashed across my mind of my mother pulling Baby Alice in her red wagon. I realized that she and Baby Alice were very close. I remembered a picture of my mother and me when I was a very little girl. I couldn't recall the details, but there was a little red vehicle in the photograph.

After the above revelation, the dream's meaning became very clear. It was a message from my inner (or higher) self that I must follow my own way, the way that had already helped me to make fantastic strides. The dream begins with the muddy road and Sy, and my insistence that we go around not straight through. I understood that it represented the prototype of the conflict between masculine linearity and female indirect intuition. It follows that the male, who is supposed to be a teacher (a staff member), is really a student in this system. The mother and daughter are making him ill at ease, and we don't care. Understandably, this wisdom leads to the memory of my close connection to my mother and an outpouring of love for her and appreciation of her life-giving gifts to me.

Intuitively I understood that Baby Alice was the link that would allow me to move ahead with my life. I became obsessed with her. I called my sister, Ruth, to ask if she would look for the photograph that I recalled among the old pictures she had in her home. When she called to tell me that she was sending out a package with some likely candidates, I could hardly control my anticipation.

In the meanwhile I became completely absorbed in my search for information about Baby Alice. The outside world had no meaning for me, so that I went about my daily tasks as if in a dream. I resented any distraction from my involvement with this subpersonality. As you will recall, Baby Alice started as a powerless, frightened little child looking out the window. Later she appeared dragging a huge hay wagon full of complaints, which were assuaged only when all the other subpersonalities assured her that they would not let people take advantage of her anymore. Her wagon then turned into a little red play wagon, which she used in a very effective way. Her most amazing accomplishment to date with the wagon had been the revitalization of Little One after she had been defeated in a battle with Mickey.

While these specific incidents give a good summary of Baby Alice's development so far, they do not completely convey the overall feeling of her personality. Her most striking quality was her quiet competence in the limited sphere of activities in which she participated. She remained fairly uninvolved with the other subpersonalities, but she watched everything that was happening and entered the fray when she was needed. Her wagon was the source of her competence. She was absolutely confident that as long as a particular problem could be solved with no more than the use of a wagon, she could handle it. She was always busy, although often only she understood what it was she was doing. Her heartwarming simplicity and complete sense of herself made her my favorite among the subpersonalities. Simply stated, I felt very good when I thought about Baby Alice.

Finally the long-awaited photographs arrived from my sister. Among them was the photo that I had remembered. I was seated on a small red wooden vehicle that I propelled by walking my legs along as I sat on the seat. Behind me on the seat sat a German shepherd puppy. What a shock! The real Baby Alice didn't have a wagon at all, she had a baby scooter. She was less attractively dressed than I remembered too. Her hair was short and straight and she wore a simple little cotton dress. This image was in sharp contrast to my pictures as a slightly older child when my mother had my hair curled and dressed me in rather fancy clothes.

The photograph both disappointed and fascinated me, and I couldn't take my mind off of it. As a result the following days were tense ones for me, and I was distant and somewhat irritable about interruptions of any kind.

Sy and I decided to make a frontal attack on the meaning that Baby Alice had for me with some visualizations. He asked me to imagine myself in the picture with the dog. The first thing I told him was that the dog was heavy on the back of the scooter and I had trouble negotiating the little vehicle with the extra weight. I was also afraid of going down the slightest incline for fear the vehicle would go too fast and I would lose control. My mother had often warned me not to scrape my new shoes on the cement sidewalk.

The scene in the visualization switched to the living room of our house, where my mother, her mother (Nana), and her brother, Teddy, were seated talking to me. Teddy was making fun of my scooter, saying that it was not as good as his wagon. The visualization then switched to the time just after Teddy's death. Baby Alice was telling her mother that she wanted Teddy's wagon. My mother told her that she was being silly because the wagon was a boy's toy not a girl's. Besides, she had already promised it to one of the boys who lived on our block.

I became very distressed after the visualization. First I began to see that life had been no picnic for Baby Alice even before the dramatic series of events initiated by Teddy's death. More than this, I now began to understand what the wagon symbolized. It was the love that Baby Alice felt she could not have, the *unconditional love* that all children need. As a child I must have understood that Teddy had a special place in my mother's heart and I longed to have that same relationship. Her love for me was always complicated by her expectations of me. Perhaps the love that my mother had for her brother seemed less complicated than this; perhaps Baby Alice believed that somehow this was associated with Teddy's being a boy.

The tension that had been inaugurated by the search for Baby Alice continued. I felt as if I were looking for pieces of a giant jigsaw puzzle and there was no telling when the next piece would fall into my hands. One day while I was waiting for my car to be repaired, I overheard the supervisor berating the mechanic who was working on my car. I became very upset by this interaction because I hate to be yelled at for doing anything wrong, and I felt sorry for the man. When my face began to twitch I became aware that some new clue might be unfolding.

When I arrived home I sat down to meditate in order to calm myself. At the end of the meditation I suddenly had a strong image of Jesus. He was walking down a path in front of me and I was trying to touch his cloak. As he turned to say good-bye to me, instead of his usual face, his face turned into a skull. It was a terrible shock and a distressing experience, which I told Didi about the next day.

During my therapy session she asked me if I would like to continue the visualization to see where it would take me. I agreed and we started. This time when I saw Jesus he was walking with the skull under his arm, followed by Baby Alice with her wagon and me. We were walking down a strange path lined with tall pikes, each of which was topped with a skull. It reminded me of stories in old English novels where kings would hang the heads of executed felons or traitors on pikes as an example to the people not to follow in their footsteps. Soon the scene changed, and Baby Alice and Jesus were walking hand in hand on a road that passed many caves.

At each cave they stopped, went in, and collected remains that they found in the caves. In some caves they found skulls, which Baby Alice brought out and placed in her wagon. In one cave they found an elephant tusk, which she was particularly pleased with and which she placed on the top of her growing pile. In the next cave it was a dog's tail, which she especially prized. She was having a wonderful time, as I could tell from her brisk stride and her enthusiastic talk. But then they had to stop because the next cave had a door that was barred.

Baby Alice became very angry at her inability to enter the cave and looked around for an instrument with which to break down the door. She grabbed a skull with ragged black hair—one that looked suspiciously like my grandmother's head—and began to pound on the door with it. She would twirl the skull around her head like a lasso and then hurl it at the door. She was angry at not being able to get in, but the process itself seemed to be great fun for its own sake. I finally had to intervene by raising the long black bar that held the door, and we all went in.

Inside the door there was a long dark hall with bats flying around and that awful smell that is associated with bats, which I remembered from Mexico. On one side of the hall there was a grotto with a pond and a waterfall. Baby Alice stopped long enough to ride down the waterfall into the pond, but then we continued on our way to the end. At the end was a large high-roofed chamber where my father sat on a raised chair, like a king. Baby Alice ran up to him and sat on his lap. They were telling jokes that I could neither hear nor understand. They kept laughing together and she was giggling. I was angry that they were ignoring me and I asked her to come along. She pulled a temper tantrum when I insisted that she had to leave, but finally came along. The last time she appeared in the visualization she was striding off with Jesus.

In discussing the images with Didi I told her that my father and Baby Alice seemed like naughty accomplices trying to lighten the burden of a household saddened by a terrible death from cancer. This visualization was like a slice of Baby Alice's past that may have been repressed, both the open hostility that would have been impossible to express and the sense of humor about the situation that would have been equally out of line.

I was getting close now to feelings that had been repressed for many years, and I couldn't stop looking. That evening I used the image of a skull and the thought of death to conjure up more visualizations. The skull dances wildly through the room, screaming in pain. Baby Alice is running around sobbing hysterically and calling for someone to come and help poor Nana. But she is yelled at and told to be quiet because her crying is making everyone even more upset. The next time I see her she is sitting under a small table in the living room, holding her knees to her chest, rocking and saying over and over again, "I hate her, I hate her, I hate her." She is very frightened.

While the visualization had revealed a specific memory about the time of my grandmother's death, my dreams took up the revelations by supplying me with general feelings from the same time period. The major elements of the dreams were: conflict that I was trying to avoid, happenings that I was trying to remember, fear that I wasn't ready for some experience.

The final image of Baby Alice in this period showed that

the visualizations were becoming clearer in meaning and revealed the integration that was taking place. One morning during my meditation what came to mind was an image of a dying elephant. Baby Alice was in the image too. She came every morning to check the elephant's condition because she was to have the tusks when the creature died. She would pull at the tusks to see if they were loosening every time she paid a visit. At the same time Little One was doing her creepy dance around the elephant. Mickey was there, too, calling Baby Alice a ghoul, but Baby Alice paid no attention to Mickey. Instead, she kept telling everyone that she was to have the tusks. It seemed that some bargain had been struck with Baby Alice a long time ago about the tusks and this time she was going to get what was coming to her.

The scene was so dramatic that I brought it to Didi to discuss that afternoon in therapy. As I related the story to her my eyes filled with tears. Sobbing between the words, I said, "Baby Alice doesn't really need those tusks anymore. All she needs now is the assurance that her needs will be met." As we closed this session I believed that I had achieved some temporary closure with respect to Baby Alice. For a while, at least, my gnawing desire to remember specific incidents relating to Nana's death seemed to be assuaged.

In the early weeks of December, Didi and I prepared for a six-week break in therapy while she took time off to have her baby. We talked about my return to the world and my growing ability to deal with people. We also knew that I was on the road to complete recovery since a recent X ray showed continued diminution of what was now a tiny spot in my chest. We sensed that the work with Baby Alice was a step in the new integration of my personality, but I'm not sure that either of us understood how the progress was being made. What I did know was that I was developing a deep attachment to Baby Alice and that I felt very good when I assumed her personality. Her independence was an important aspect of her personality and indicated that she operated in a mode possibly created before language and certainly without the benefit of rational explanations or understanding. I knew that her obsession with death was important to her and would just have to work its way out in the future. It was becoming clear to me that she was playing a pivotal role in my new integration, although I did not yet understand all of its ramifications.

With the advantage I have from writing this book, I think that I have a clearer picture of what was happening. I had begun this period with the insight that in order to complete my recovery, I had to advance into a positive gear, not just get rid of my negativity. My fear of success, the fear that it would trigger malevolence from those in my environment, was the major impediment to achieving this goal.

I discovered through fantasy that Baby Alice was the key to my freedom if I could understand her symbolism and her needs. I learned that her red wagon was a substitute for the wagon that had belonged to my mother's dead brother and that she had always coveted. The wagon was a symbol of male superiority and of the unconditional love that she had as an infant but had lost. She used the wagon to collect skulls, bones, and especially the tusks of a dying elephant. In doing this she was taking for herself the male birthright to succeed and wresting power from the grandmother, whom she saw as the origin of the concept that males were superior.

Ironically, having accomplished this feat, she began to realize that the tusks themselves were not necessary to have. She learned that real power for her (and for me) lay in being authentic and following our unique source of power in female intuition and spiritual healing. The most important exercise in authenticity was to face Baby Alice's true feelings toward my grandmother at the time of her death, to remember that she was frightened by Nana's screams and was insulted by the unfair criticism directed to her childish expressions of distress. She remembered that she hated Nana as a result.

In essence I was beginning to reconstruct the core of my personality based on authentic emotional reactions and on the assurance that some part of me could get my permission to succeed. The memory of my early emotional link to my mother gave Baby Alice a solid platform from which to begin development anew. She, alone of all my subpersonalities, could ignore the bad parts of the mother/daughter relationship that developed as I grew up because she had experienced the very strong love of my mother for me as her first child and the object of her early and undivided affection. As my sister put it recently, "No matter what else happened between you and Mother, Alice, we all knew that she loved you very much."

I must emphasize that this period in which we began to unravel the mystery of Baby Alice was only a beginning. It remained for the lessons learned here to be absorbed by the other parts of my personality. The theme of male superiority and the self-permission to succeed had to be worked out with other subpersonalities in many forms before the issue was dropped.

As if to underscore the end of this period of therapy, I awakened one morning to a wonderful surprise. As I looked out of my bedroom window at the pond, I saw that it was snowing. At first I was as excited as ever that the ground was covered with white. But then a flood of emotion enveloped me. I remembered that day back in June when I took as my goal to survive to see one more snowfall. I stood at the window sobbing softly because this was the first snow, and I had lived to see it.

15

Love at Last

The paths of old reactions remained in my mind even after they had been bypassed by new, healthier roads. It took a long time for them to be reforested and forgotten. I returned to therapy in February after a hiatus of two months, not with any pressing issues to discuss but with an understanding that I was not yet well, not yet whole. I knew that if I neglected the all-important finishing touches, I would not get rid of the tiny tumor that remained in my lung. Or that I might succumb to a new illness sometime in the future. I had to free myself of the negativity that lingered in the background, to sweep away the seeds of some new bloom of self-destruction

Little by little I handled each of the remaining areas of concern. The Mickey part of me was impatient to be on the move again, to try to find a new career. I think she was trying to distract herself from the change that she saw coming, change that would involve finally giving up her cherished emotional reactions. Both Sy and Didi kept telling me not to jump into any commitments before I was ready, to let the inner-healing process unfold. My intuition told me the same thing. Over and over I dreamed of being helpless, experiencing great upheavals, but then seeing new vistas revealed. While Mickey kept fighting the inevitable, I felt agitated and slightly depressed.

All of my feelings of jealousy and guilt came to a head soon after I returned to therapy. We learned that Marty's mother-in-law had to return to the hospital again to have another cancerous growth in her mouth removed. We were stunned because we believed she was on the way to complete recovery after successful surgery three months before. I had reacted personally to her illness when it was first discovered just after Marty's wedding. I had been very jealous of her when we met because she was so beautiful and accomplished. When she became ill I was devastated because some part of me felt that my jealousy had caused her illness. The reaction passed as she seemed to be recovering, but now it was back.

This episode was Mickey's last hurrah, her last attempt to control my reactions by intense jealousy followed by guilt. Didi assuaged the guilt by assuring me that my thoughts could in no way have influenced Marty's mother-in-law. Baby Alice helped by being very nice to Mickey and telling her that she would help her. But the real understanding came slowly. I understand now that the dreams of helplessness reminded me that the source of the jealousy/guilt were the childhood threats to my most simple needs. The dreams of overcoming obstacles that led to dramatic change told me that I needed to be strong in the world. Although I never conceptualized the idea overtly that my jealousy/guilt would abate as I became more assertive in the real world, that is the way it happened.

Marty's mother-in-law did not recover from her illness. The whole family was terribly saddened by her death in November of the same year. It was an ironic twist of fate that the woman whom I had so admired and envied was gone while I continued to live. It was a bitter lesson to me to appreciate what I was and what I had. I felt anger and a sense of unfairness, but I did not turn the anger on myself. My grief did not keep me from being happy to be alive and proud of myself. Mickey was secure at last.

The slow change in Mickey was a sharp contrast to the dramatic resolution of Baby Alice's problem with Nana. Baby Alice was in many ways the most secure part of my personality. Her growing ability as conciliator showed her pivotal role in the integration of all aspects of my self. But what would happen when the issue involved a weakness in Baby Alice? Who was there to help her? I soon discovered that I had hidden sources of wisdom and strength.

The most obvious source of unresolved negative feelings was the intense hatred of Baby Alice for Nana. To summarize, in various visualizations Baby Alice had manifested unbridled hostility toward Nana, from banging her detached skull against a stone wall, coming to get tusks from a Nana-like dying elephant, to direct expression of hatred for her because of the commotion surrounding her final illness. I knew that this had to be settled so we faced the issue directly. Didi's strategy was to ask me to visualize myself as Nana. I assume she felt that this would elicit some sympathy toward her that we could use to change Baby Alice's attitudes.

The strategy worked. After an initial success with being Nana. I quickly switched to being myself and talking about her in an understanding way. I told Didi that I understood that the loss of her son, Teddy, was a terrible blow for her. I said that I understood how she felt about Baby Alice, that Baby Alice took too much of her own daughter's time, and that everything Baby Alice did seemed to annoy her. I told Didi that I had a slightly more positive feeling toward Nana as a result of the visualization. It seemed that we were making progress.

Neither of us had anticipated the counterreaction of Baby Alice. The next day in my meditations I had to face an irate Baby Alice, who was furious. She was pacing up and down, muttering that she had been betrayed by our discussion and that both Didi and I had been taken in by Nana. Baby Alice was shouting that Nana was a liar, had been bad-mouthing poor Baby Alice for her whole life, and that Baby Alice was completely justified in all of her hostility to Nana. She went on and on until I became exhausted with the intensity of her emotions.

I sat down quietly and tried to calm poor Baby Alice. As I pictured her in my mind, Bagera, the tiger, who was her special friend, came to take her for a ride on his back. I thought it was strange, but Bagera took her to see villages that had been devastated by fire. Baby Alice did not witness the actual fires but just the resulting devastation—smoldering huts, crying children, and gaunt-faced adults. Bagera seemed to know what he was doing because he forced her to look even though she did not want to. The tiger told her that she had to look at the scene or she would turn into Mickey. This was such a terrible threat that Baby Alice managed to look at the scene, although to soften the effect, she kept her hands over her eyes. For some reason known only to Bagera, this did calm her down and she went off laughing on the back of the tiger as he carried her into some nicer places as well.

It was obvious to me that this visualization was of great importance. If I could trust the message from my higher wisdom, as expressed in the tiger's understanding, it seemed that the Mickey part of my personality had been formed and separated from the Baby Alice part when I was forced to deal with my reactions to my grandmother's death. To find out more about this we tried another visualization in order to look directly at my grandmother's death.

I visualized the house at that time and the room where I
know my grandmother slept. I found Mickey in the hall
near Nana's room trying to run past the door and down the
stairs without looking in. Something stopped her, however,
and she paused outside to listen. Her breathing began to
come in short breaths as she could hear Nana herself struggling for air and in great pain. I started to sob as I recalled
this image and I, too, could not get my breath. With this
physical reaction came great sympathy for Nana, but from
Mickey, not from Baby Alice.

Baby Alice was there, too, in the visualization but she
refused to enter the room or stay in its vicinity. Late one
night, however, she came back to the room riding on
Bagera. She said that she knew Nana was suffering and that
it was because of all the bad things Nana had done to Baby
Alice. She had no sympathy at all, but she was very afraid
of Nana. In a low voice she said that she was not going to
let Nana hurt her and that she would fight her to the finish
if she had to so that Nana would not come back and take
her with her when she died.

Didi and I talked about this schism in the attitudes of
Baby Alice and Mickey to Nana and how it was formed by
a child's inability to handle all of the intense and contradic-
tory feelings toward a sick and dying grandmother. I was
left with a sense of confusion followed by an intense sense of
anxiety and foreboding.

It was so physically uncomfortable to bear this feeling
that I meditated and tried to form an image of what I was
experiencing. I imagined other times when I had the same
feeling—usually when I was alone at night and unable to
ignore ominous sounds that signaled the presence of hostile
ghosts or worldly intruders. Suddenly I had an image of a
little girl dressed in white sitting along the road with a calculator in her hand, very busily recording everything that

was going on. She told me that her name was Mousey. She was a twin to Baby Alice in appearance, but her manner was completely different. Where Baby Alice was confident, she was fearful; where Baby Alice acted on her own secret motivation, Mousey was bombarded by the events in the outside world. Her main complaint was that she could not handle the demands that were being placed on her, demands that she was forced to continually calculate.

The best way to describe my condition at this time was one of overstimulation—every sound was like a blast in my ears and every touch was painfully intense. Sy tried to help me, but I resented both the sound of his voice and the idea that he was trying to make me talk about my feelings. One day I rested by alternatively sleeping and reading, but I was still tense and had a bad headache. Finally, in the evening, I agreed to try to deal with the feelings and got back into the image of Mousey. This time she was in my grandmother's room, but Nana wasn't there. She was walking around the room looking for her and sobbing that she had lost her dear Nana and she didn't know where she had gone. It was the first time in a long while that I was so overcome with such an intense emotion, and this release made me feel a little better. Sy wanted to pursue the flow of such positive concern about my grandmother from Mousey, but by now I was exhausted and just wanted to sleep.

That evening I dreamed that we were in a car at a border crossing. I was a little kid and was told that the authorities should not be given certain information that we were carrying on the floor of the car, but a border guard eventually got it all out of me. While I still don't understand this dream completely, the images of being at an important crossover place and revealing to the authorities something that was supposed to be kept quiet is pretty clear.

By the next day the tension that I had been experiencing

began to have more physical ramifications. I had an intense pain along the stitch line of my incision, something that I had never experienced before. At about eleven o'clock I sat down to meditate, and when I was finished I tried another visualization. I saw an awful scene of Mousey surrounded by a pack of rats, crying and again mourning the loss of her dear Nana. Some of the rats were attached to her side along the line of my scar. There was a snake that was keeping the rats at bay. Mousey had a crazy thought that as long as the snake could keep away the rats from her side, she could still love Nana, despite the deep hurt that she felt because Nana had left without saying good-bye.

This image did not quite hang together logically, but I had the idea that it somehow was terribly important to me at the time of my grandmother's death and my sister's birth to handle the combination of intense love, hate, and guilt toward Nana. As a six-year-old child I could not put it all together. Therefore, parts were walled off and I learned to adopt a way of being in the world that at least kept me going. As a result Baby Alice retained the cold anger toward Nana, Mickey feel guilt toward her, while Mousey had a strong regret that she was gone. I believe further that Baby Alice probably made a pact with herself never to trust or love anyone ever again after Nana left and betrayed her. Mousey, on the other hand, retained the sense of being overwhelmed with a situation that she felt she could not control and vowed she would never be taken by surprise again. Hence her compulsive need to record and calculate everything she saw.

The most interesting part of all this is that both the bad events and the good feelings were forgotten, and that the feelings of love were the last things to be remembered, perhaps because they would have made Baby Alice feel too vulnerable.

Writing this now gives me some fresh insights into the guilt, love, and hate triumvirate that so concerned me. I do not know what the snake stands for, but the rats are, I believe, self-castigation and guilt because I felt angry with Nana and probably wished for her to die. The lesson is that if I can control the guilt, I can feel both love and the pain of separation and rejection. In other words, the guilt tends to confuse and blind me. If I don't feel responsible for her death, then I can say, "Yes, I loved her *and she loved me.* Yes, she left without saying good-bye, but that is the way these things happen. It is no one's fault." However, when I feel guilty I think, *How could I have loved her if I wanted her to die so that the house would be calm again?* Or I think, *She somehow knew how I felt and so it is no wonder that she left and didn't say good-bye.* In other words, the fact that she didn't say good-bye means that she knew about me and was punishing me. If I hated her, it was because she hated me and deserved the hostility that I felt toward her.

This explanation makes it clear to me also why the love was the last thing to come out because love makes the relationship so much more complicated. As a child, the feelings of hatred and guilt were preferable to those of love and a feeling of loss, no doubt because the former gave me quicker integration. If my case is typical, it would appear that love may too often be the victim of the strong human need to seek closure. At any rate, without this understanding, just being able to emotionally acknowledge the love at last helped me to make my peace with Nana.

My confidence in my present interpretations is strengthened by the fact that the focus of my thoughts and therapeutic work in the following weeks was about a new model of relationships. Instead of seeing everyone as all good or all bad, I understood that each person has both good and bad in them. With this idea as a background, I was ready for the assault on the last barrier to my integration—my relationship to my father.

In the days that followed I felt somewhat more positive toward my father. But then one morning I awakened with a slight feeling of nausea. When I tried to meditate to get rid of the feeling, I found that a visualization was interfering. Baby Alice and Mousey were fighting about who my father was. I then saw Baby Alice and Mousey approaching a door that was being blocked by my father. Baby Alice told him to get away because she was coming through. Baby Alice then walked off with Mousey and told her that she had to get rid of that goddamned calculator, but in return she, Baby Alice, promised to take in more day-to-day information.

After these experiences I had the impression that by telling my father off, Baby Alice was clearing the final barrier for me to be able to succeed in the world and that perhaps I had always sensed that I didn't really have my father's permission to do so. The result of all this activity was that I felt good about myself and was able to have some strong meditations. I ended the day with an affirmation that I would release myself into perfect health and happiness and that all I needed to succeed would come to me.

In the next few days I got closer and closer to some final settlement with my father. The stimulus came from a dream in which there was a doomed man for whom all hope for reprieve was exhausted. I did not kill him, but by failing to make a call, the process went on and I knew that he was dead.

The meaning of the dream was very clear to me. It referred to the day that my father died. He was very ill we knew, and the doctor had come on the day before to look at him. I stayed in his room with him at night sleeping on a chair. When I awakened early in the morning I noticed that his breathing had taken on a strange rattling sound that I immediately related to stories of a death rattle just before one dies. My sister and I called for the doctor to come, but when he did not arrive we decided to call the emergency ambulance as well. However, soon after we had made the call, he stopped breathing. By the time they arrived he had been dead for almost a half hour.

We both felt that we should have called the ambulance sooner and felt responsible for his death. The ambulance drivers made us feel somewhat better by telling us that they didn't see many cases of old people dying in their own homes with their family around them the way he did. And when the doctor finally came he also said that he had died in the best way. I thought that I had lost the feeling of guilt about this incident, but this dream told me that it was not so.

The weeks passed quickly for me now as we moved into the final stage of therapy. There were still things to be discussed about my father. I remember a whole session in which my task was to try to look at the bad things about him. It was amusing to discover that every criticism I made of him was immediately neutralized by a "but" statement in some way presenting some excuse or balancing good trait that he had. Strange that he turned out to be the most enigmatic of all the people close to me, and the most complicated. This is probably because he, like me, made a lifetime career of not being frank and honest about his needs and desires. I can only assume that he was always like this and that I had a hard time understanding him from the beginning.

Shortly after this session I had a dream that was rather unique in its subject matter but gave me unusual feedback on my progress in dealing with this last stumbling block to wholeness. I dreamed that I had lost some important data from my dissertation. I was searching for it near a long low building. Suddenly the building collapsed. First the foundation crumbled and then the roof descended slowly to the ground. There was a hand sticking out of the rubble (palm down) but before my eyes it turned to cloth.

This dream was a conundrum when I recorded it, and because my entries in my diary were getting briefer and briefer, I just let it pass. Now, however, I suspect that it was telling me that I was making peace with the image of my father, that I was at last realizing that my impression of my relationship with him was false. My first association to the dream elements was to a movie called *The Fallen Idol.* It was about a little boy who loses his innocent admiration of a father figure after finding him in a compromising situation. The second association was to the house that fell in *The Wizard of Oz.* The house with the hand sticking out of it was reminiscent of the scene in which Dorothy's house falls on the Wicked Witch of the East, leaving only her feet and her shoes sticking out.

This dream, then, represents my search for something important that I have lost—not my dissertation, but the relationship with my father. The building collapsing expresses the fact that the old feelings of admiration for him have collapsed, leaving only the hand, which turns to nothing. It is the recognition that the image of him as an idol is over and that if I think about our relationship, I will realize that it never was as close as I wanted it to be.

My father was a warm, attentive, and generous man who loved his family very much. I thought that I was his favorite, but I now know that it was my mother whom he loved the most, and my sister with whom he shared interests and values. I think that we both made demands on each other that were impossible to satisfy, and we became annoyed with each other in the process. He wanted me to share his standards, which I could not do; I wanted him to support

me against my mother, which was asking too much of him.
We did love each other very much, but the love was tainted
by these unreasonable expectations. As with Mickey, I did
not need to forgive him, I only needed to release the love for
him that was always there. Now, and only now, I could do
it.

June 1986 brought the incredible news that my X rays
were "normal." There was no trace of the lung tumor. As
before, the news required time to completely assimilate and
it did not result in either elation or calmness. But I knew
that these results also signaled that I should be thinking
about ending therapy with Didi.

At the beginning of the next hour I told Didi that I had
decided to stop therapy for the summer because we would
both be going away, and I thought it would take the pressure off of us. She responded that she preferred to end therapy for now and if I wanted to return in the fall, we would
start anew. That way, she said, I would be under no obligation to come in September or even to contact her if I didn't
want to. We spent our last hour together talking about the
whole process. I told her that she had been a flawless therapist for me. I said that the most important gift she gave to
me in the relationship was her loving but uninvolved approach. She is the only person I have known well who never
made demands on me to perform. If things went well for
me, I knew that she would be happy, but if I died, I knew
that she was prepared to let me go. I had only to take care
of myself, not her as well, and I needed that very much.

She, for her part, told me that she was terrified when we
began because Sy had such high expectations of the therapy.
But once she set our sights away from physical healing to
psychological wholeness, she was fine. She admitted that
before she first saw me, she had gathered all of the books on
the mind/body relationship that she could find but had read

none of them. Something made her reject all of this information for confidence in her own ability to react to me and make up the rules as we went along. Of course this was just right: She gave me the skeleton of the procedure and together we took it from there.

It was a short session, and we parted as we had so many times before. We hugged each other in the hallway of her home, I patted Flash, the dog, for the last time, and I walked out of the door. Neither of us looked back and we have rarely seen each other since.

16

What Ever Happened to Baby Alice?

It is now May 1989 and it is light-years away from my last entry in my journal in time as well as spirit.

It has been a time of continual improvement for me. The effects of therapy have been long-lasting for both my physical and emotional well-being. Although to my casual acquaintances I may not appear markedly changed, my inner experience of the world is very different. I handle life situations much better than before, and I do not allow myself to be in situations where people take advantage of me. As a result, the bouts of depression that used to come out of nowhere have disappeared. Occasionally, I feel moments of the intense anger and hostility that used to plague me, but they pass quickly. It is in these moments from another time that I realize how far I have come and how much I have changed.

My greatest pleasure in the past year has been writing this book. For once in my life I have been involved in a project that I enjoyed for the process as much as for the final product. It has been most challenging for me to try to conceptualize how I became ill and what it was that saved me. I have written this "just for me," and that is important in itself.

Before the final word is said, however, there is a question that I must handle. What ever happened to Baby Alice and her friends as my life returned to normalcy? As always with Baby Alice, the answer is unpredictable and completely out of my rational control.

For many months after the termination of therapy I continued to meditate and visualize the breakup of the cancer cells in all parts of my body. The visualization would begin with the gathering of all the subpersonalities at the spaceship pad. First Amanda, the builder, would arrive and stride up the gangplank in her sturdy shoes. She was dressed, as usual, in her tan overalls and pretty cotton blouse, with her tawny, thick blond hair falling down to her waist. She was in charge of the mechanical working of the ship and she would turn on all of the control lights and examine the ship's engines. Amanda never spoke. She worked in silence and exuded a calm competence.

Athena, the subpersonality who was my wise guide, came next. She never came from the parking lot, but arrived from a side entrance. She was dressed incongruously in her flowing white robes and battle helmet. She was the navigator. She would enter the ship, remove her helmet, and begin to work on the course for the day.

Following these two early arrivals came Mickey. Who could miss her, with her flame-red curly hair, her purple eyes, and green dress? By this time she had grown up from the *Annie* look-alike to an attractive, mature woman. I was pleased by her metamorphosis because I assumed that as an adult she would be more responsible. Mickey, of course, was the captain of the enterprise and assumed her place in the captain's seat in front of the flashing control board. She, like the other two, paid attention to her own job, and there was no interaction among them.

Little One arrived in one of two manners, depending on

whether she came as herself or as Bagera, the tiger. If she arrived in her usual leotard dancing outfit, she would often come from below the middle of the gangplank and jump up into the ship near the door. Since she didn't have a specific job, she would look around and then choose someplace to perch and watch the others. But if she were in her tiger form, she would arrive in a grand manner, pause at the entrance, look around as if to say, "No one would dare to challenge me," and then proceed to walk up the entryway with her lumbering, confident stride. She would also survey the whole operation as she entered, and then also take a place on some upper ledge to observe, half asleep but ever on guard.

The quiet, concentrated activity in the ship would continue until the entrance of Baby Alice, who would come on the scene pulling her red wagon. Baby Alice, of course, is still a little kid. She has straight, shiny, light brown hair cut short, and she wears her white cotton dress very short. Each day she would park the little vehicle neatly outside and walk in accompanied by Mousey, with calculator in hand, riding her rhinoceros. Baby Alice and Mousey would invariably engage in some sort of heated argument, which would be picked up by the rest. "Leave the smelly animal outside!" they would all yell, but Mousey would defiantly ignore them and proceed to the place that had been set aside for the creature. There was some sort of stall that had been built into an indentation in the side wall. Mousey would arrange the bedding hay with care and make sure the animal had enough to drink. Then she would close the chicken-wire door and take her place beside Baby Alice at the source of a healing ray.

The last one in was Oriole, who would fly in quickly, chirping, "Blast off, blast off," and the ship would be on its way. Rising vertically in a cloud of smoke, the ship would circle up and over the landscape until it came to the image of myself displayed on the ground. Carefully, and with pass after pass, Baby Alice would concentrate the ray on my chest, disintegrating any vestige of the lesions that had been there. Eventually my whole body would be enveloped in light, and then I would usually try to forget the spaceship and concentrate on the rest of my meditation.

This process continued unchanged for months, even when the length of my meditations got shorter and their number decreased to one a day. Then one day something changed. As the group gathered on the pad waiting for Baby Alice and Mousey to arrive, I noticed a red flash of color in the parking area. It was a red sports car. Out of the car stepped a young woman dressed stylishly in white, with shoulder-length brown hair cut bluntly and turned up at the ends. As she slammed the door authoritatively I could see her face. It was not pretty but it was rather a nice face that gave the impression of beauty because of its health and enthusiasm. She strode energetically up the gangplank, followed by Mousey and Tara, the rhino.

I gasped inwardly as a pain caught up my chest in a terrible moan. Then I realized rationally what was happening: It was Baby Alice all grown up. Much as I was pleased with the maturity of my other subpersonalities, it was not so for Baby Alice. Somehow I expected her always to remain a little kid. Much as I tried, however, to bring back the image of her as a child, it would not come. She remained grown up. For several days after this event tears would come to my eyes when I thought of her, and it was terrible not to be able even to talk to her.

Then one day I watched the spaceship return, which in itself was a very unusual event. Before she could get into her car I asked her to talk to me and explain her new life. She told me that she was very busy with a husband and two

small children (twin boys) at home. She pretty much told
me that I didn't need her anymore because the things that I
had to figure out could not be solved with a wagon, and I
knew that she was limited in this respect. She was perfectly
nice, but as always she had her own agenda and was eager
to return to it.

A few mornings later I sat at the breakfast table telling Sy
how devastated I was at the loss of Baby Alice. He didn't in
any way make fun of the ludicrous story I was telling him
but instead just looked at me and said, "You know, don't
you, Alice, that the fact that she has grown up means that
you have integrated her into your personality and so she is
still with you." I told him through my silent tears that I
knew this was true but the hurt and loss were still there.
And then, as if suddenly struck with how silly this all must
sound, we both broke into laughter.

Once or twice later I tried to contact Baby Alice to help
me with some issue that I was dealing with. At these times
she was more patient and understanding, but she reiterated
her message that it was not something she could help me
with and that I should contact some of my other subpersonalities. Sometime later the whole spaceship stopped flying because the healing beam now emanated from a small
metal sphere that Mousey carried in her pocket. I had
watched as the grown-up Baby Alice had presented this
sphere to Mousey, who now was to be in charge. It seemed
that she had been willed all of Baby Alice's healing power,
which now was concentrated in this sphere.

It didn't occur to me to try to understand all of this when
it was happening, but as I write now I have some understanding of the attraction for me of the Baby Alice personality. She was the epitome of childish innocence in that she
saw the world in limited terms, all of which she believed she
could control. Like a kitten or a young puppy that has com-

pletely conquered its environment and doesn't know about the things that can hurt it in the outside world, Baby Alice was secure and confident. Besides, she had magical gifts that exist nowhere but in fairy tales. The adult can never have that kind of confidence because he/she knows that the world is capricious, unfair, and unpredictable. But although we cannot know our world completely, we hope to be able to adjust to whatever we cannot control.

I guess that it was necessary for me to experience the extreme confidence of a Baby Alice in order not only to heal myself but also to create a new personality from the ashes of the old one. But that aspect of myself is not appropriate for me now because the emphasis between the needs of my inner and outer lives has completely switched. Then my inner life was very complicated while my outer social life was kept purposely primitive. It was okay for me to have a personality that was asocial and intuitive since I had only myself and my family to satisfy. But now my inner life has faded into the background and my outer life is more complicated and so I need to be more rational and responsible for my actions. Besides, as Baby Alice surmises, my problems are with little anxieties, not with basic reorganization, and it is Mousey who needs to be tapped and developed, not she. I also still have Mickey and Little One/Bagera to rely on, and in an emergency there is always steady Amanda.

Oh, yes, I almost forgot. I really don't need Baby Alice anymore for another reason. Last Christmas, Sy bought me the most beautiful red wooden wagon that I have ever seen. It is a constant reminder of the power of my fantasy and the power of the mind to heal.

PART

IV

Afterthoughts

A book is more than the sum of its pages because insights occur in the process of writing that were absent at the beginning. This final section describes some of my beliefs about how, in my case, the mind worked its wonders to heal.

THE FOUR DIMENSIONS OF THE HEALING MIND

My experience was unusual in its four-dimensional approach to psychological and physical health. I have described the rational methods that I used to put my experiences into perspective, the fantasies that I created to reach my preconscious mind, the dreams that I interpreted to contact unconscious material, and the spiritual paths that I followed in learning how to manifest health.

I used my rational mind throughout therapy. It was involved in my assumption that a cancer-prone personality existed, that I fit its description, and that I might extend my life if I could change what I believed to be harmful attitudes. I made a rational decision to try alternative methods of healing when traditional methods were exhausted. My rational mind was involved in discussing strategies, recording notes in my journal, assessing progress, and making rational integrations. However, this part of the mind did not orchestrate the healing by itself, nor did it always know where the process was going.

The second dimension that I employed was the spiritual, the realm of faith and of union with the universal. I believe that the belief of my therapist, Didi, in the transpersonal aspect of the psyche created an environment that was all-important for me. The spiritual work I did helped to reverse my illness because I needed some catalyst to rouse me from my deep emotional rut. Our reactions to the world are based on well-established ways of interpreting events that become automatic. It is therefore difficult to take a radically different perspective while we are caught in the grooves of old ways of thinking. By taking a spiritual approach one is able to suspend the normal views of the world and relate to it in a different way. I operated on a completely different level of understanding when I meditated, recited my affirmation, and tried to reach the universal part of myself. I was in an altered state of being where time slowed down and life's goals became elevated. However, I believe that meditation alone would not have sufficed. The specific methods on manifesting health that I learned from Yogananda and David Spangler were necessary additions to my ordinary meditation practice. I needed the additional impetus of intense faith in my recovery that these philosophies brought to me.

The most unusual aspect of my healing mind occurred at the preconscious level, the realm of fantasy and visualization. According to S. Epstein this part of the mind automatically interprets and copes with events according to generalizations derived from emotionally significant experiences. Often these generalizations are in the form of visual and tactile images that may be organized into complex constellations, as in the case of my subpersonalities. I believe that the information that came to me from my subpersonalities could have been accessed in no other way in the limited time that we had to work. They allowed me to find the source of my moods and of some of my sensitivities and compulsions in my relationships to the significant people in my life. The fantasies also revealed the special characteristics of the preconscious mind. Once begun, the fantasies took on a direction of their own, in modes beyond my conscious control and often beyond my understanding. But each fantasy taught me a lesson and the lessons put me on the road to health.

The final dimension that I tapped was the realm of dreams and the unconscious. My dreams were helpful in passing on to me images from broad feelings about my progress in finding synthesis, my status in life, the sense of being blocked or proceeding smoothly, and from information that was repressed. I interpreted my dreams using only my immediate associations and some general help from Didi and Sy. I followed no standard book of interpretations. Sometimes I understood the meaning of the dream at the time it occurred, but often it was only later that its full meaning became manifest.

Overall, I believe that the power of the healing force was multiplied more than four times by the use of these dimensions in a synergistic process that literally worked a miracle.

ELEMENTS OF THE HEALING PROCESS

There are many different theories of how the mind influences the body to heal. Some say that the essence of the process is faith; others believe that forgiveness is the all-important ingredient; still others believe that self-love is the vital clue. I think that all of these elements plus some others are important and that they may play specific roles at different times in the healing experience. What follows is a discussion of those ingredients that I think were important to me.

COMMITMENT TO CHANGE—BEGINNING THE HEALING JOURNEY

The first part of any journey is the decision to begin, to make a change. I decided to attempt a psychological approach to my illness only after being told that standard medical avenues would not be effective. Once I decided on psychosynthesis, I dedicated myself to the therapy in all ways. I attended my therapy sessions twice a week and read all of the assignments that Didi suggested. On my own I followed a strict meditation schedule, and I visualized the cancer cells in my body diminishing. I believed that my attitudes to life and my destructive way of being in the world were responsible partly for my illness. Although psychological wholeness, not physical well-being, was the goal of therapy, we believed that if I could change my attitudes, I would be able to extend my life.

A strange bonus accrued to me when I decided to engage my illness directly. The decision was accompanied by a feeling of power and independence, and was important in reversing the feeling of helplessness and dependency that was the essence of my cancer-prone personality. It also signified a strong stand for life. Although I often would tell Sy that I didn't want to die, I frequently could not give him a good reason for me to live. One of the turning points in my psychological–spiritual path of healing was my realization that life was more important to me than my husband, my family, or any aspect of the way I was living. I told myself that if someone offered me life at the cost of leaving my home and never again seeing my loved ones, I would opt to go. I would opt to live. I am convinced that my dedication to myself was an essential ingredient in my final recovery.

SELF-LOVE—SUSTAINING THE HEALING

Once the process of regeneration began, it had to move forward and be maintained. I believe that the development of self-love played an important role in the continuation of the curative process. In the two-week period after we discovered that the lung lesion was diminishing, I began to identify aspects of myself that I could not love. These characteristics were summarized in the jealous, insincere, ambitious, and energetic subpersonality named Mickey. She had sent me on the road to the Ph.D., and I literally believed that "she" was trying to kill me. The day I realized that I could not leave her and truly loved her was an important turning point in my recovery. I believe that the intense feeling of transformation and unity that I felt as a result of feeling love for this hated part of myself spurred on my recovery.

Beyond the initial need to learn to love the most negative part of me, the development of self-love was important in reversing the negativity in my personality. Some therapies for cancer patients emphasize the use of general self-loving techniques throughout the healing process. But this was not the case with psychosynthesis. Instead, Didi surrounded me with love by supplying me with a warm and respectful atmosphere. It was not the kind of love that was expressed by much talk of loving but was shown in a deep respect for me, for my ideas, and confidence that my higher self existed and could be trusted to lead both my therapist and me. She also helped me to appreciate the sources of love that were all around me in the love of my husband, my family, my parents and friends, and she encouraged me to try to love all of my subpersonalities. I could monitor the development of self-love in the changes in my attitude to the subpersonality, Baby Alice. As she was transformed from a whimpering, helpless little waif into a competent woman, I went from being annoyed with her, to admiring her, and finally to having a deep attachment to her. I felt a warm glow inside me when I thought about her, no matter what she did or said.

Without actually stating it in so many words, the theory and practice of psychosynthesis gave me the kind of environment that I had lacked as a child. I consider this the most precious gift that I received in the process of my healing.

REVERSING THE CANCER-PRONE PERSONALITY— ESSENCE OF THE PROCESS

Once the cancer was turned around and the healing process was maintained, months of work remained in retraining my way of being in the everyday world. I think that it is useful to conceptualize this work as the reversing of the cancer-prone personality as it had developed in me, that is, rebuilding the hollow self. By being motivated to please others instead of myself, I had established patterns of thought and behavior that turned love for others into insecurity, accomplishment into failure, and empathy into pain. These habits of processing information inhibited the development of the core of my self-confidence. Clearly this way of thinking needed to be reversed.

Sy and I had always been aware that I thought categorically, superstitiously, and emotionally. Instead of processing events so that they would have a minimal impact on my emotional well-being, my thoughts tended to make me more frightened and less powerful. Didi, too, realized that I was a poor thinker, not logically but practically, to make myself happy. She specifically reacted to the way I processed the world, working in general to turn my destructive thinking into a more constructive way of reacting to life's experiences. She taught me to enjoy the process as well as the goal; to remember that all things are transient and that I should not obsess over any one occurrence. She taught me to be strong in the world, to develop my will, and to satisfy my needs directly. She encouraged me to develop my own standards, not to take those of others. I believe that all of the above worked to develop my independence and to eliminate my feelings of helplessness and hopelessness.

My emotional independence brought with it an additional bonus: I could establish more mature and enjoyable love relationships. Just as dependence and fear of rejection had made loving painful to me, independence allowed me to relate to others in a more honest way and to enjoy the positive aspects of love. Part of this conversion was the work that we did on changing my models of the world. I gave up my desire for a perfect mother and for a husband who would always agree with me and anticipate my every need. I was amazed at how many preconscious concepts I had about the way things should be, and how unhappy it made me when these dreams were not actualized. When I actually examined these assumptions and their ramifications, I understood that the reality would not have pleased me at all. But more important, as long as I could satisfy my needs directly, I did not require unrealistic, overcompensating dreams.

Didi specifically helped me to reverse the processes of the hollow self with respect to achievement. She taught me directly how to transform my desires into accomplishment that I could accept and respect. She started by teaching me that I could find out what I wanted by accessing my higher self. Part of the knowledge that I needed became available through the training of my intuition and some of it came through the wishes and desires of my subpersonalities. A part of every routine of creating a subpersonality was to ask, "What does this person want?" We also worked directly on realistic goal-setting, such as trying to live to see another snow. When the snow finally came and I was still alive, I was proud of my accomplishment because it had been a reasonable goal and I had worked so hard to achieve it.

Another step in reversing the hollow self was to reduce my extreme empathy to others. We worked on this with general techniques of shielding myself from stimulation and by changing certain behavior patterns. I often suffered unreasonably with others because I believed that I had brought on their calamities by wishing them ill. Once I could acknowledge my hostility, be convinced that some of it was justified, and learn to stand up for myself, I didn't feel it anymore. This in turn reduced my feelings of guilt, my need to punish myself by feeling the pain of others or my need to do something to allay their pain. I also stopped apologizing for myself and thus stopped eliciting criticism and unwanted advice from others.

There were other patterns, not described by the hollow-self metaphor, that had to be broken. I had to rework specific sensitivities and compulsions to significant others that resulted in moods of sadness, helplessness, and hostility. My subpersonalities helped with this. By allowing the volatile subpersonality called Little One to express her feelings in fantasy, I was able to understand my extreme guilt reactions toward my sister and my sexual desires toward my father that had created moods of agitation and feelings of hostility.

By allowing Baby Alice to collect skulls and express direct death wishes to my dead grandmother, I found the origin of my feelings of worthlessness, guilt, and anger. Or, in the very beginning of therapy, visualizing my reactions to a picture that I had drawn about my mother and me, allowed me to identify and reduce the hurt that I felt about my mother.

The most exciting aspect of this part of therapy is that I was able to rid myself of feelings that I had experienced over a lifetime in a matter of months and sometimes weeks. It appears that, in my case at least, direct emotional catharsis such as yelling, shouting hostile epithets, pounding pillows, or excessive crying was not necessary. Instead, by allowing my subpersonalities to express even more extreme behaviors directly in fantasy, the strong emotions faded away. Once the initial fantasies of direct expression were over, what my subpersonalities wanted more than anything else was the acceptance of their way of viewing the world. Baby Alice was assuaged of her feeling of injustice (her hay wagon full of wrongs) by being assured that she had good reason to feel badly treated and that it would not happen again. Little One's jealousy was abated when her needs were acknowledged and I made her a promise to integrate her. I have no idea how common this use of fantasy is or how it may apply in other cases. For me fantasy was a direct road to my significant emotional experiences and led eventually to the cessation of my many unpredictable moods.

SYNTHESIS—THE ULTIMATE GOAL

The ultimate aim of my therapy was not health but unity or wholeness. These goals were attained not by ridding myself of unwanted aspects of my personality but by creating a synthesis out of the disparate parts. Sometimes this was achieved by elevating various aspects of self by taking them up the mountain. In this way the destructive Little One found an alternative form as Bagera, the tiger. As a tiger she manifested kindness and incredible wisdom. Bagera understood, for instance, that in order for Baby Alice to love her grandmother, she had to be willing to face the pain associated with losing her. By the same method, the pathetic crab, who yearned to be a flying horse, was transformed into a happy and beautiful oriole. As a result I turned hopelessness and unreasonable desire into a beautiful but practical goal.

In other ways opposites were identified and brought to agreement. I had many direct conflicts between my subpersonalities with respect to issues such as dependency versus independence and evaluation of my relationship to my father. I had overall problems with sensuality and spirituality, which I discovered were opposite aspects of passion. A final way that synthesis occurred was in changing my categorical, guilt-ridden thinking into a more modulated view of the world, which allowed for more happiness and understanding. Also, by jettisoning my ideal models of the world, there was less conflict between what was and what I believed the world should be.

Unlike the dramatic effects of self-love or spiritual leaps, the effects of integration were manifested slowly over almost a year more in therapy. They were seen most dramatically in the way my subpersonalities learned to help each other. Baby Alice could help Mickey when she was afraid of imminent change in my life and was able to explain to Little One that I could have the power of a boy without actually being one. In turn, Little One, in her tiger form, helped Baby Alice understand about the complications of loving and forgiving her grandmother. Unity was also manifested in my ability to forgive and express love for certain family members that had been restrained for years. The expression of love was the final manifestation of synthesis.

ARE ATTITUDES DANGEROUS TO YOUR HEALTH?

The concept of a cancer-prone personality is controversial, I believe, because it is hard to accept the fact that attitudes can affect our physical well-being. I, myself, rejected my husband's warnings about the seriousness of my self-negativity. Despite clear evidence that I fit the cancer-prone description, and a history of cancer among my close female relatives, I did not believe that it would happen to me. I used to joke about the fact that I was a nonconstructive thinker, and I thought it was funny when I got the highest grade possible in a test on nonexpression of hostility. Needless to say, I have mended my ways. I believe that my attitudes were partly responsible for both my illness and my recovery.

I am optimistic that the psychological precursors of cancer may become more accepted by laymen and physicians alike in the future because research in this area is moving forward at an accelerated rate. For instance, recent studies on lung cancer showed that attitudes such as hopelessness and a tendency to shun quarrels explained more of the incidence of lung cancer than did smoking. As a matter of fact, this study showed that cancer was related to smoking only in people who had the appropriate cancer-prone type of personality. Other studies have shown that there is hope for the prevention of cancer through behavior therapy to change attitudes. Single studies as well as single case histories can neither prove nor disprove the existence of a cancer-prone personality. However, the day may come when attitude-changing therapy is an accepted part of treatment for cancer.

I know that many physicians reading this book will think that my change in attitude had nothing to do with my recovery, that it was one of the rare cases of spontaneous remission that do occur. I doubt this interpretation to be true because my illness was getting worse before I started psychological therapy, and because statistics show that what happened to me occurs less than four in one thousand times for patients with metastacized kidney cancer. At any rate, we may discover someday that "spontaneous remission" often is synonymous with spontaneous changes in attitude, and we may be able to make it a more common occurrence.

THOUGHTS ABOUT LIFE AND DEATH

My battle with cancer was one of the most significant experiences of my life. Besides the innumerable changes that I have described, its most lasting effect is a dramatic change in my attitude toward living. Before I became ill I assumed that I would live to be about eighty years old. On every birthday I would sadly note the diminishing number of years that I had left. Now, however, I celebrate each birthday as a triumph that I have lived to experience another year. It is a shame that it took a life-threatening illness to bring about this change, but I am grateful that I have learned at last to appreciate the gift of life.

Bibliography

Butterworth, E. *Discover the Power Within You.* New York: Harper & Row, 1968.

Castenada, C. *Tales of Power.* New York: Simon & Schuster, 1974.

Cousins, N. *The Anatomy of an Illness.* Toronto: W.W. Norton, 1979.

DeVita, V.T., Jr., S. Hellman, and S.A. Rosenberg. *Cancer: Principles and Practice of Oncology.* Philadelphia: J.B. Lippincott Publishing Co., 1985.

Epstein, S. "The Implications of Cognitive-experiential Self-Theory for Research in Social Psychology and Personality." *Journal for the Theory of Social Behavior,* Vol. 15:3, Oct. 1985, pp. 283–310.

Epstein, S. "Cognitive-experiential Self-Theory: Implications for development psychology." In M. R. Gunner (Ed.), *Self Process in Development, Vol. 23.* Minnesota Symposium on Child Development, 1989.

Evans, E. *A Psychological Study of Cancer.* New York: Dodd, Mead, 1926.

Eysenck, H.J. "Personality as a predictor of cancer and cardiovascular disease, and the application of behavior therapy in prophylaxis." *European Journal of Psychiatry,* Vol. 1 (1987), pp. 29–41.

Eysenck, H.J. "The Respective Importance of Personality, Cigarette Smoking and Interaction Effects for the Genesis of Cancer and Coronary Heart Disease." *Personality and Individual Differences.* Vol. 9, No. 2, pp. 453–64. Printed in Great Britain: 1988.

Ferrucci, P. *What We May Be.* Los Angeles: J.P. Tarcher, 1982.

Firman, D., and J. Firman. *Mothers and Daughters.* New York: Firman Associates, nd. (out of print)

Firman, Julie and Dorothy. *Daughters and Mothers: Healing the Relationship.* New York: Crossroad/Continuum, 1989.

Glassman, J. "They Beat Cancer." *Family Circle,* Feb. 24, 1981.

Goleman, D. *The Meditative Mind.* Los Angeles: Jeremy P. Tarcher, Inc., 1988.

Grossarth-Maticek, R., R. Frentzel-Beyme, and N. Becker. "Cancer risks associated with life events and conflict solutions." *Cancer Detection and Prevention,* Vol. 7 (1984), pp. 201–209.

Le Shan, L. *You Can Fight for Your Life.* New York: Evans, 1977.

Livingston-Wheeler, V. *The Conquest of Cancer.* New York: Franklin Watts, 1984.

Middleton, R.G. "Surgery for metastatic renal cell carcinoma." *Journal of Urology,* Vol. 97 (1967), pp. 973–977.

Nolen, W.A. *A Surgeon's Book of Hope.* New York: Berkley Books, 1982.

Pelletier, K. *Mind as Healer, Mind as Slayer.* New York: Delta Books, 1980.

Rogers, C. *Client Centered Therapy.* New York: Houghton Mifflin, 1951.

Sallitaro, J.S. *Recalled by Life.* New York: Avon Books, 1982.

Siegel, B. *Love, Medicine, and Miracles.* New York: Harper & Row Publishers, 1988.

Simonton, C., S. Matthews-Simonton, and J. Creighton. *Getting Well Again.* New York: Bantam, 1980.

Spangler, D. *The Laws of Manifestation.* Moray, Scotland: Findhorn, 1981.

Synthesis Center Staff. *Psychosynthesis-Conscious Evolution.* Amherst: The Synthesis Center, nd.

Yogananda, P. *Autobiography of a Yogi.* Los Angeles: Self-Realization Fellowship, 1985.

Yogananda, P. *Scientific Healing Affirmations.* Los Angeles: Self-Realization Fellowship, 1981.